TECHNICAL JAPANESE SUPPLEMENTS
James L. Davis, General Editor

Solid-State Physics and Engineering

Craig T. Van Degrift

Kanji-Flash Softworks

The University of Wisconsin Press

University of Tokyo Press

Preface

　　This book is intended as a companion to the textbook *Basic Technical Japanese*, by E. E. Daub, R. B. Bird, and N. Inoue, University of Wisconsin Press and University of Tokyo Press (1990), which will be referred to hereinafter as "BTJ." Its purpose is to provide a systematic guide for learning the KANJI needed for reading technical materials in solid-state physics and engineering. After an introductory review lesson (Lesson 0), there are 10 lessons, each of which features 10 KANJI; by the end of the book you will be very familiar with these additional 100 KANJI. Also, a small number of important KANJI pairs are presented; each of these pairs is best learned as a single entity. These 100 KANJI and 14 KANJI pairs, along with the 365 KANJI presented in BTJ, will give you a firm basis for doing technical reading and translation of articles, books, and reference works in the solid-state field.

　　The KANJI featured in this book were selected by going through all the entries in the indexes of キッテル固体物理学入門 (translated by 宇野良清, 森田章, 津屋昇 and 山下次郎) and 半導体超格子の物理と応用 (edited by the 日本物理学会), and selecting those KANJI, not in BTJ, that form words essential for reading in the solid-state field. Preference was given to KANJI that form many compounds, that form compounds with KANJI in the BTJ list of 365, or KANJI whose opposites are to be found in the BTJ list.

　　This book may be used in either of two ways: (i) it may be studied after you have gone through all of BTJ; or (ii) it may be studied concurrently with BTJ. The lessons are designed so that you may, if you wish, begin to use this book when you are starting Chapter 11 of BTJ. The chapters of BTJ and the lessons of this book have the following correspondence:

Chapters in BTJ:	1-10	11	12	13	14	15	16	17	18	19	20
Lessons in this book:	0	1	2	3	4	5	6	7	8	9	10
Page numbers in this book:	1	3	13	21	29	39	45	53	65	75	85

Thus, in Lesson 2 you are expected to know all the KANJI and grammar rules given in the first 12 chapters of BTJ. It will be necessary for you study all 20 chapters of BTJ; although the final chapters deal with biology and physiology, they still introduce a number of KANJI useful in solid-state physics and engineering.

　　Each lesson begins with a list of 10 KANJI along with their meanings and readings; very large KANJI are included so that you may photocopy them and make KANJI cards if you wish. The KANJI page is followed by a list of solid-state-related words and technical terms that can be formed with these KANJI and those up through the corresponding chapter in BTJ; a supplementary list of solid-state physics-related words that can be formed with the BTJ KANJI is also included.

These lists should be studied carefully in order to understand the various ways that the KANJI are used to construct technical words. Study of these words also provides a good review of KANJI learned up to this point. After this, there are various exercises designed to confront you with all 10 KANJI of the lesson in a variety of settings. By the time you have finished the lesson you should have become quite familiar with the 10 new KANJI; you will also have had the opportunity to review some grammar points as well. For the most part the sentences and paragraphs have been taken, often with some modification, from the following sources in addition to the books mentioned above:

西村久訳; "量子ホール効果"; シュプリンガー・フェアラーク東京 (1989)

福山秀敏, 石川征靖, 武居文彦; "セミナー高温超伝導"; 丸善 (1988)

菊池誠; "半導体の話"; NHKブックス (1968)

宮脇; "半導体回路"; 電気書院 (1964)

"応用物理" 58, No. 4; 応用物理学会 (1989)

The readings frequently contain KANJI not yet studied; these are indicated with an underline, just as in BTJ, and their readings are given. You need make no special effort to learn these underlined KANJI when you encounter them. Most will appear in later chapters and lessons, and you should learn them there. When going through the chapters in BTJ and the lessons in this book, concentrate on learning the KANJI being featured in the chapter or lesson and learn them thoroughly. These KANJI will cover about 93% of the KANJI found in the solid-state literature.

Three appendices have been included to assist in locating the KANJI and vocabulary presented in this book. Appendix A presents supplementary vocabulary that, while not particularly technical, are commonly found in technical literature. Included are a bonus list of 14 additional KANJI and 20 additional KANJI pairs, together with 83 other words that appeared in the exercises. Appendix B lists the ON and KUN readings of all featured KANJI and KANJI pairs, and Appendix C contains additional solid-state physics vocabulary involving KANJI not presented formally in this book. Learning the vocabulary of the appendices will increase your KANJI "hit rate" to about 97%. The remaining KANJI are found largely in proper names and non-technical phrases. This book follows the conventions and notation adopted in BTJ. For the rules on parentheses, brackets, hyphens, and so on, please consult pp xiii to xv of BTJ.

A number of colleagues examined the manuscript for this book and suggested useful changes. These colleagues include Professor R. Byron Bird of the University of Wisconsin-Madison, Dr. Ken Lunde of Adobe Systems, Inc., Dr. Mitsuru Tanaka of the National Research Laboratory for Metrology, Tsukuba, Japan, Mr. Mitsuo Fujita of Daicel Chemical Industries, Ltd., Ms. Junko Mori of the University of Wisconsin-Madison and Ms. Hana Tateishi of the University of Wisconsin-Madison. The author is especially grateful for the patient and extensive assistance of the series editor, Professor James L. Davis of the University of Wisconsin-Madison.

Craig T. Van Degrift
Kanji-Flash Softworks
PO Box 3119
Gaithersburg, Maryland 20885-3119

October 1994

KANA REVIEW

In this lesson you have the chance to review KANA and to acquire some additional vocabulary needed for reading about solid-state physics and engineering. This exercise can be completed after reading Chapter 3 of *Basic Technical Japanese*.

Ex. 0.1 Words written entirely in KATAKANA

Cover the English translations with a piece of paper. Read the Japanese KATAKANA words aloud and then translate them.

アルカリハライド	alkali halide	アルミニウム	aluminum
アンチモン	antimony	ナトリウム	sodium
カリウム	potassium	セシウム	cesium
マグネシウム	magnesium	ダイヤモンド	diamond
グラファイト	graphite	シリコン	silicon
シリサイド	silicide	ゲルマニウム	germanium

インジウムアンチモン	indium-antimonide
トリフェニルメチル	triphenylmethyl
ハイゼンベルク・モデル	Heisenberg model
バーガース・モデル	Burgers model
アインシュタイン・モデル	Einstein model
クローニッヒ・ペニーのモデル	Kronig-Penny model
k·pハミルトニアン	**k·p** Hamiltonian
パーコレーション	percolation
デバイ・モデル	Debye model
ウィグナー・サイツ・セル	Wigner-Seitz cell
K-セル	K-cell
バーガース・ベクトル	Burgers vector
エネルギーギャップ	energy gap
エネルギーバンド	energy band
バンドエネルギー	band energy
フェルミ・エネルギー	Fermi energy
ポテンシャルエネルギー	potential energy
クーロン・ポテンシャル	Coulomb potential
レナードジョーンズのポテンシャル	Lennard-Jones potential
ベクトルポテンシャル	vector potential

マーデルンク・エネルギー	Madelung energy		
バンドギャップエネルギー	band gap energy		
ギンツブルグ・ランダウ・パラメーター	Ginsburg-Landau parameter		
フォトルミネセンス	photoluminescence		
フォトルミネセンススペクトル	photoluminescence spectrum		

ソフトモード	soft mode	ナイト・シフト	Knight shift
バンドのずれ	band shift	ブリルアン・ゾーン	Brillouin zone
ブラッグ・ピーク	Bragg peak	サテライト・ピーク	satellite peak
リコンストラクト	reconstruct	ダングリングボンド	dangling bond
ドーピング	doping	スペーサ	spacer
アクセプター	acceptor	ドナー	donor
ホール	hole	バンドギャップ	band gap
ホールバンド	hole band	ミニゾーン	mini-zone
ミニバンド	mini-band	サブバンド	sub-band
アモルファス	amorphous	アモルファスシリコン	amorphous silicon
スピネル	spinel	ガラス	glass
カルコゲンガラス	chalcogen glass	メットグラス	Metglas
クラスタ	cluster	アロイクラスタリング	alloy clustering
ルビーレーザー	ruby laser	オプトエレクトロニクス	optoelectronics
メーザー	maser	ネオジムガラスレーザー	neodymium glass laser
プラズモン	plasmon	ソリトン	soliton
フォトン	photon	フォノン	phonon
プラズマ	plasma	ヘリコン	helicon
ポーラロン	polaron	ポラリトン	polariton
ランダウ・ゲージ	Landau gage	スペクトロメーター	spectrometer
クリープ	creep	g-マーカー	g-marker
ドメイン	domain	フラキソイド	fluxoid
ホイスカー (or ウイスカー)	whisker	エントロピー	entropy
アーク	arc	スパッタ・エッチ	sputter etch
チャネリング	channeling	デチャネリング	de-channeling
トレーサー	tracer	ガンダイオード	Gunn diode

因	イン	cause; factor
格	カク；コウ	frame; standard
規	キ	standard
孔	コウ あな	hole hole
衡	コウ	balance beam, scales
思	シ おも（う）	thinking, thought to think
指	シ さ（す） ゆび	indicating, pointing to indicate, point finger
純	ジュン	purity
砒	ヒ	arsenic
負	フ お（う）	burdened; negative to bear (a burden)

因 格
規 孔
衡 思
指 純
砒 負

因

因果律	インカリツ	causality
因子	インシ	factor
起因	キイン	cause, origin
原因	ゲンイン	cause, origin
デバイ・ワラー因子	デバイ・ワラーインシ	Debye-Waller factor

格

ウィグナー格子	ウィグナーコウシ	Wigner lattice
規格	キカク	standard
格子	コウシ	lattice, grating
格子エネルギー	コウシエネルギー	lattice energy
格子間位置	コウシカンイチ	interstitial position
格子定数	コウシテイスウ	lattice constant
斜交格子	シャコウコウシ	oblique lattice
正格子	セイコウシ	direct lattice
体心立方格子	タイシンリッポウコウシ	body-centered cubic lattice, bcc
単位格子	タンイコウシ	unit cell
単純立方格子	タンジュンリッポウコウシ	simple cubic lattice, sc
電子格子	デンシコウシ	electron lattice
二次元斜交格子	ニジゲンシャコウコウシ	two-dimensional oblique lattice
ブラベ格子	ブラベコウシ	Bravais lattice
平衡格子定数	ヘイコウコウシテイスウ	equilibrium lattice constant
格子並進操作	コウシヘイシンソウサ	lattice translation operation
面心立方格子	メンシンリッポウコウシ	face-centered cubic lattice, fcc

規

規格	キカク	standard
規則	キソク	rule, standard
規則合金	キソクゴウキン	ordered alloy
規則・不規則変態	キソク・フキソクヘンタイ	order-disorder transition
規定する	キテイする	to prescribe
ノルドハイムの規則	ノルドハイムのキソク	Nordheim's law
ヒューム・ロザリーの規則	ヒューム・ロザリーのキソク	Hume-Rothery rule
不規則合金	フキソクゴウキン	disordered alloy
フントの規則	フントのキソク	Hund rule
マティーセンの規則	マティーセンのキソク	Matthiessen's rule

孔

重い正孔	おもいセイコウ	heavy hole
正孔	セイコウ	positive hole
電子・正孔対	デンシ・セイコウツイ	electron-hole pair

衡

化学平衡	カガクヘイコウ	chemical equilibrium
熱平衡状態	ネツヘイコウジョウタイ	thermal equilibrium conditions
平衡	ヘイコウ	equilibrium, balance
平衡格子定数	ヘイコウコウシテイスウ	equilibrium lattice constant
平衡蒸気圧	ヘイコウジョウキアツ	equilibrium vapor pressure
平衡方程式	ヘイコウホウテイシキ	equilibrium equation

思

ローリンの思考実験	ローリンのシコウジッケン	Laughlin Gedanken (thought) experiment

指

指向性	シコウセイ	directional
指数関数	シスウカンスウ	exponential function
指定する	シテイする	to specify
方向を表わす指数	ホウコウをあらわすシスウ	direction index
面指数	メンシスウ	Miller indices
有理指数	ユウリシスウ	rational index

純

アクセプター不純物	アクセプターフジュンブツ	acceptor impurity
純	ジュン	purity
純金	ジュンキン	pure gold
純度	ジュンド	(degree of) purity
単純立方格子	タンジュンリッポウコウシ	simple cubic lattice, sc
ドナー不純物	ドナーフジュンブツ	donor impurity
不純物	フジュンブツ	impurity, impurities

砒

ガリウム砒素	ガリウムヒソ	gallium arsenide
砒素	ヒソ	arsenic

負

正負	セイフ	positive and negative, ±
負数	フスウ	negative number

SUPPLEMENTARY VOCABULARY USING DEDICATED KANJI PAIRS

The KANJI that form these pairs will rarely be seen separately in solid-state physics material. They are more easily remembered as pairs.

井戸	いど	well
多重量子井戸	タジュウリョウシいど	multiple quantum well
多重量子井戸レーザー	タジュウリョウシいどレーザー	multiple quantum well laser
多重量子井戸レーザーダイオード	タジュウリョウシいどレーザーダイオード	multiple quantum well laser diode
単一井戸	タンイツいど	single (potential) well
単一量子井戸	タンイツリョウシいど	single quantum well
単一量子井戸レーザー	タンイツリョウシいどレーザー	single quantum well laser
二重結合電子井戸	ニジュウケツゴウデンシいど	double-bonding electron well
ポテンシャル井戸	ポテンシャルいど	potential well
量子井戸	リョウシいど	quantum well
量子井戸細線	リョウシいどサイセン	quantum well wire
量子井戸箱	リョウシいどはこ	quantum well box
量子井戸レーザー	リョウシいどレーザー	quantum well laser
降伏	コウフク	yield
降伏応力	コウフクオウリョク	yield stress

SUPPLEMENTARY VOCABULARY USING KANJI FROM CHAPTER 11

渦糸状態	うずいとジョウタイ	vortex state
改正	カイセイ	revision
ガラス状シリカ	ガラスジョウシリカ	vitreous silica
強結合モデル	キョウケツゴウモデル	tight-binding model
強弱	キョウジャク	relative strength
ギンツブルグ・ランダウ方程式	ギンツブルグ・ランダウホウテイシキ	Ginsburg-Landau equation
ゲージ不変性	ゲージフヘンセイ	gage invariance
コラム状成長	コラムジョウセイチョウ	columnar growth
最初の	サイショの	the first, initial
サイクロトロン周期	サイクロトロンシュウキ	cyclotron period
周期的ポテンシャル	シュウキテキポテンシャル	periodic potential
修正したリュードベリの式	シュウセイしたリュードベリのシキ	modified Rydberg equation
シュレーディンガー方程式	シュレーディンガーホウテイシキ	Schrödinger equation
状態数	ジョウタイスウ	number of states
振動子強度	シンドウシキョウド	oscillator strength
段丘状階段	ダンキュウジョウカイダン	terrace step
電子の運動方程式	デンシのウンドウホウテイシキ	electron equation of motion

トーマス・フェルミの近似	トーマス・フェルミのキンジ	Thomas-Fermi approximation
二次元量子状態	ニジゲンリョウシジョウタイ	two-dimensional quantum conditions
ファイバー光学	ファイバーコウガク	fiber optics
ブロッホ発振器	ブロッホハッシンキ	Bloch oscillator
ブロッホ方程式	ブロッホホウテイシキ	Bloch equation
ポアソン方程式	ポアソンホウテイシキ	Poisson equation
ホールの運動方程式	ホールのウンドウホウテイシキ	hole equation of motion

(*Note*: Hole and Hall are the same in KATAKANA.)

マクスウェル方程式	マクスウェルホウテイシキ	Maxwell's equations
ラウエ方程式	ラウエホウテイシキ	Laue equation
ラグランジュ運動方程式	ラグランジュウンドウホウテイシキ	Lagrange equation of motion
量子補正	リョウシホセイ	quantum correction
リング発振器	リングハッシンキ	ring oscillator
ロンドン方程式	ロンドンホウテイシキ	London equation

EXERCISES

Ex. 1.1 Matching Japanese and English terms

( ) 井戸　　　　　( ) 思考実験　　　　　( ) 不純物
( ) 規格　　　　　( ) 正負　　　　　　　( ) 平衡格子定数
( ) 原因　　　　　( ) 電子・正孔対　　　( ) 面指数
( ) 降伏応力　　　( ) 不規則合金　　　　( ) 砒素

1. arsenic　　　　　　5. equilibrium lattice constant　　9. (potential) well
2. cause, origin　　　　6. Gedanken experiment　　　　　10. standard
3. disordered alloy　　　7. impurity　　　　　　　　　　11. Miller indices
4. electron-hole pair　　8. plus or minus　　　　　　　　12. yield stress

Ex. 1.2 Choosing the correct KANJI

Here are some pairs of KANJI that are somewhat similar in appearance or that have a common radical. Form meaningful JUKUGO, give the KANA transcriptions and translate.

Example:
　　　　(1)心　　(2)応　　　　中(1) チュウシン center　　(2)力 オウリョク stress

1.　(1)度　(2)原　　　　( )因　　　　　　温( )
2.　(1)比　(2)砒　　　　( )重　　　　　　( )素
3.　(1)測　(2)則　　　　規( )　　　　　　( )定
4.　(1)正　(2)生　　　　( )孔　　　　　　( )成
5.　(1)井　(2)化　　　　( )学　　　　　　( )戸
6.　(1)結　(2)純　　　　( )合　　　　　　( )度
7.　(1)衡　(2)行　　　　平( )　　　　　　( )程
8.　(1)使　(2)指　　　　( )数　　　　　　( )用
9.　(1)格　(2)相　　　　( )子　　　　　　固( )

Ex. 1.3　Matching Japanese technical terms with definitions

Read each definition carefully, and then choose the appropriate technical term. Words that you have not yet encountered are listed following the definitions.

（　）因果律	（　）熱平衡状態	（　）格子間位置
（　）重い正孔	（　）単純立方格子	（　）不純物
（　）降伏応力	（　）有理指数	（　）規則・不規則変態
（　）平衡蒸気圧	（　）多重量子井戸	（　）電子の運動方程式

1.　ある合金の低温での規則状態から高温での不規則状態への転移。
2.　純物質中の望ましくない異物。
3.　全部分が、系の周囲と同じ均一温度に達している系の状態。
4.　有効質量が大きいホール。
5.　ある時刻における系の力学状態と周囲との相互作用を指定すれば、その後のすべての時刻の系の状態と、その状態で任意の力学変数を観測して得られる値に対する確立分布が定まるという原理。
6.　結晶格子の原子の間の位置。
7.　物質の二つ以上の相が平衡状態で共存している系の蒸気圧。
8.　引張り実験片の伸びが荷重の増加なしに増加しはじまる最小応力。
9.　単位セルが立方体で、格子点が立方体の各頂点に位置する結晶格子。
10.　一つ以上のポテンシャルエネルギーの極小がある超格子。
11.　時間の関数として、電子の位置を規定する方程式。
12.　結晶面の型を指定する3個の整数。

低温	テイオン	low temperature	結晶	ケッショウ	crystal
転移	テンイ	(phase) transition	共存する	キョウゾンする	to coexist
望ましい	のぞましい	desirable	引張り	ひっぱり	stretching
系	ケイ	system	片	かた	fragment
周囲	シュウイ	surroundings	伸び	のび	extension
均一	キンイツ	uniform	荷重	カジュウ	(applied) load
達する	タッする	to attain, reach	各-	カク-	each
有効	ユウコウ	effective	頂点	チョウテン	vertex
時刻	ジコク	time, occasion	極小	キョクショウ	minimum
相互作用	ソウゴサヨウ	interaction	超-	チョウ-	super-, ultra-
任意の	ニンイの	arbitrary	型	かた	model
観測する	カンソクする	to observe	個	コ	parts, pieces
値	あたい	value	整数	セイスウ	integer
確率分布	カクリツブンプ	probability distribution			

Ex. 1.4 Sentence translations

Read each sentence aloud several times and then translate it. You will encounter some KANJI that you do not yet know, but the words using these KANJI are listed following the sentences.

1. 理想的な結晶は、一定の構造単位を、空間に限りなく繰り返していくことによって形成される。
2. 銅、銀、金、鉄、アルミニウム、アルカリ金属のような最も簡単な結晶では構造単位は1個の原子である。
3. 3次元の点群対称性により表1に示す14個の異なった格子型が必要となる。
4. 体心立方格子の基本単位格子を図11に示し、基本並進ベクトルを図12に示す、面心立方格子の基本並進ベクトルを図13に示す。
5. 定義に従えば、基本単位格子は1個の格子点しかもたないが、通常の体心立方単位格子は2個の格子点をもち、面心立方単位格子は4個の格子点をもっている。
6. これら格子型は7種の型の単位格子によって分類された結晶系、すなわち三斜晶系、単斜晶系、斜方晶系、正方晶系、立方晶系、菱面体晶系、六方晶系に類別される。

理想的な	リソウテキな	ideal	基本-	キホン-	primitive, fundamental
結晶	ケッショウ	crystal	図	ズ	figure, drawing
構造	コウゾウ	structure	並進	ヘイシン	translation {movement}
空間	クウカン	space	定義	テイギ	definition
限りなく	かぎりなく	without limit	に従って	にしたがって	according to
繰り返す	くりかえす	to repeat	通常の	ツウジョウの	conventional, usual
形成する	ケイセイする	to form	種	シュ	kind, variety
銅	ドウ	copper	三斜	サンシャ	triclinic
銀	ギン	silver	単斜	タンシャ	monoclinic
鉄	テツ	iron	斜方	シャホウ	orthorhombic
金属	キンゾク	metal	正方	セイホウ	tetragonal
簡単な	カンタンな	simple	立方	リッポウ	cubic
点群	テングン	point group	菱面体	リョウメンタイ	rhombohedral
対称性	タイショウセイ	symmetry	六方	ロッポウ	hexagonal
異なる	ことなる	to differ from	類別する	ルイベツする	to classify as

Ex. 1.5 Paragraph translations

Read each paragraph aloud several times and then translate it. You will encounter some KANJI that you do not yet know, but the words using these KANJI are listed following the paragraphs.

1. 結晶の対称操作は、結晶をそれ自身に重ね合わせる。これらには格子並進操作が含まれている。さらに、点群操作といわれる回転操作と鏡映操作とがある。すなわち格子点あるいは単位平行六面体の中の特別の点に関して、回転操作や鏡映操作を行って結晶をそれ自身に重ね合わせるのが可能なことがある。

2. 結晶面の位置と方向とは、その面上の一直線上にない3点によって決定される。もし各点が異なった結晶軸上にあるならば、それらの点の座標を格子定数a_1, a_2, a_3を単位

として与えることにより、結晶面を決定することができる。しかし、結晶構造解析には次に示す規則により決定された指数によって面の方向を表す方が便利である。

1: 面が結晶軸を切りとる長さを、格子定数a_1, a_2, a_3を単位として表す。この結晶軸は基本格子のものでも非基本格子のものでもよい。

2: これらの数の逆数を求め、同じ比をなす3個の整数に、通常は最小の整数に簡約する。その結果を括弧でくくって(hkl)とし、これをその結晶面の面指数という。

3. ダイヤモンド構造の特徴である正四面体結合を図に示す。各原子は4個の最隣接と12個の第2隣接原子をもっている。ダイヤモンド構造は他の構造にくらべて隙間が多い。すなわち剛体球を置いて満たすことのできる体積の割合は最大で0.34にしかすぎず、面心立方構造あるいは六方最密構造のような最密構造の充填率の46%である。ダイヤモンド構造は、元素の周期表の第4列にある原子の指向性共有結合による構造の例である。

操作	ソウサ	operation {math}	整数	セイスウ	integer
自身	ジシン	self-	簡約する	カンヤクする	to simplify
重ね合う	かさねあう	to superimpose, to map	括弧	カッコ	parentheses
			特徴	トクチョウ	characteristic
回転	カイテン	rotation	正四面体	セイシメンタイ	regular tetrahedron
鏡映	キョウエイ	reflection			
平行六面体	ヘイコウロクメンタイ	parallelepiped	隣接	リンセツ	adjacent
			第2	ダイニ	second, next
特別の	トクベツの	special	他の	タの	other, another
可能な	カノウな	possible	隙間	すきま	gap, interstice
決定する	ケッテイする	to determine	剛体球	ゴウタイキュウ	rigid sphere, hard sphere
軸	ジク	axis			
座標	ザヒョウ	coordinate	満たす	みたす	to fill (up)
与える	あたえる	to give	割合	わりあい	role
解析	カイセキ	analysis	最密構造	サイミツコウゾウ	closest-packed structure
便利	ベンリ	convenient			
切り取る	きりとる	to cut out	充填率	ジュウテンリツ	filling factor
非-	ヒ-	non-			
逆数	ギャクスウ	inverse (number)	列	レツ	column
求める	もとめる	to obtain, get	共有	キョウユウ	covalent, shared

Translations for Ex. 1.4

1. An ideal crystal is formed by repeating a fixed unit structure without limit through space.
2. The structural unit for the simplest crystals, like those of copper, silver, gold, iron, aluminum, and the alkali metals, is a single atom.
3. The 14 different lattice types shown in Figure 14 are required by three-dimensional point-group symmetry.
4. The primitive cell of a body-centered cubic lattice is shown in Figure 11, and its primitive translation vectors are shown in Figure 12. The primitive translation vectors for a face-centered cubic lattice are shown in Figure 13.
5. According to the definition, a primitive unit cell has no more than one atom per lattice point, but the conventional body-centered-cubic unit cell has two lattice points and the face-centered-cubic unit cell has four lattice points.
6. These lattice types are classified into lattice systems according to seven kinds of primitive lattice types, i.e., triclinic, monoclinic, orthorhombic, tetragonal, cubic, trigonal and hexagonal.

Translations for Ex. 1.5

1. Crystal symmetry operations map a crystal onto itself. These can include lattice translation operations. In addition, there are the so-called point-group operations: rotation operations and reflection operations. Specifically, there is the possibility of mapping a crystal onto itself through rotation and reflection operations around lattice points or special points within a primitive parallelepiped.

2. The position and direction of a crystal face can be defined by three non-collinear points in the face. If each point is on a different crystal axis, it is possible to specify the crystal faces by giving the coordinates of those points using the lattice constants a_1, a_2, and a_3 as units. However, in crystal structure analysis it is convenient to express the surface directions in terms of indices which can be determined according to the following rules:
1: Express the length to the point where the surface cuts the crystal axis in units of the lattice constants a_1, a_2, and a_3. These crystal axes may be those for either primitive or non-primitive cells.
2: Obtain the reciprocals of these numbers and reduce them to three integers that have the same ratios, usually the smallest integers. When those are enclosed in parentheses as (hkl), they are called the Miller indices of that crystal face.

3. Tetrahedral bonds, which are a characteristic of the structure of diamond, are shown in the figure. Each atom has four nearest neighbors and twelve next-nearest neighbors. Compared with other structures, the diamond structure has a great deal of open space; the proportion of its volume that can be filled by hard spheres is at most only 0.34, which is 46% of the filling factor of the closest-packed structures—the face-centered cubic structure or the hexagonal closest-packed structure. The diamond structure is an example of a structure formed by the directional covalent bonds of atoms of the fourth family of the periodic table of the elements.

12

域	イキ	region
引	イン ひ (く)	pulling, attraction to pull, attract
軌	キ	orbit; track
区	ク	domain; section, division
軽	ケイ かる (い)	light (in weight) light (in weight)
斥	セキ	repelling
走	ソウ はし (る)	running; scanning to run; to scan {xu-verb}
道	ドウ みち	road; course; way path {math}
領	リョウ	territory
励	レイ	encouragement, stimulation

域 軌 軽 走 領

引 区 斥 道 励

域

固有温度領域	コユウオンドリョウイキ	intrinsic temperature range
地域	チイキ	region, zone
領域	リョウイキ	region, domain

引

引力	インリョク	attractive force
引き上げる	ひきあげる	to raise, pull up

軌

軌道	キドウ	orbit, orbital
軌道の量子化	キドウのリョウシカ	quantization of orbits
結合軌道モデル	ケツゴウキドウモデル	bond-orbital model

区

磁区	ジク	magnetic domain
区分	クブン	classification

軽

軽い正孔	かるいセイコウ	light hole
軽量材	ケイリョウザイ	lightweight material

斥

斥力のポテンシャル	セキリョクのポテンシャル	repulsive potential

走

走行時間	ソウコウジカン	transit time
チャネル走行時間	チャネルソウコウジカン	channel transit time
ブロッホ振動走行	ブロッホシンドウソウコウ	Bloch oscillation transition

道

軌道	キドウ	orbit, orbital
軌道の量子化	キドウのリョウシカ	quantization of orbits
結合軌道モデル	ケツゴウキドウモデル	bond-orbital model
道筋	みちすじ	path

領

固有温度領域	コユウオンドリョウイキ	intrinsic temperature range
要領	ヨウリョウ	gist, purport
領域	リョウイキ	region, domain

励

室温励起子	シツオンレイキシ	room temperature exciton
弱結合励起子	ジャクケツゴウレイキシ	weak-bonded exciton
素励起	ソレイキ	elementary excitation
二次元励起子	ニジゲンレイキシ	two-dimensional exciton
フレンケル励起子	フレンケルレイキシ	Frenkel exciton
モット・ワニエ励起子	モット・ワニエレイキシ	Mott-Wannier exciton
励起子	レイキシ	exciton
励起状態	レイキジョウタイ	excited state
励磁電流	レイジデンリュウ	magnetizing current

SUPPLEMENTARY VOCABULARY USING A DEDICATED KANJI PAIR

The KANJI that form this pair will rarely be seen separately in solid-state physics material. They are more easily remembered as a pair.

永久	エイキュウ	permanent, persistent
永久磁石	エイキュウジシャク	permanent magnet

SUPPLEMENTARY VOCABULARY USING KANJI FROM CHAPTER 12

k空間	kクウカン	k-space
アーバック過程	アーバックカテイ	Orbach process
還元ゾーン形式	カンゲンゾーンケイシキ	reduced zone scheme
球のプラズマモード	キュウのプラズマモード	spherical plasma mode
空格子近似	クウコウシキンジ	vacant lattice approximation
空格子点	クウコウシテン	lattice vacancy
空格子点対	クウコウシテンツイ	lattice vacancy pair
原子形状因子	ゲンシケイジョウインシ	atomic form factor
光電子放出	コウデンシホウシュツ	photoemission
磁化	ジカ	magnetization
周期的ゾーン形式	シュウキテキゾーンケイシキ	periodic zone scheme
消衰係数	ショウスイケイスウ	extinction coefficient
単位胞	タンイホウ	unit cell
反磁場係数	ハンジばケイスウ	demagnetization coefficient
反磁性体	ハンジセイタイ	diamagnet
反射係数	ハンシャケイスウ	reflection coefficient
ランジュバンの反磁性方程式	ランジュバンのハンジセイホウテイシキ	Langevin diamagnetic equation

EXERCISES

Ex. 2.1 Matching Japanese and English terms

( ) 固有温度領域　　( ) 空格子近似　　( ) 単位胞
( ) 原子形状因子　　( ) 電子軌道　　　( ) 領域
( ) 光電子放射　　　( ) 走行時間　　　( ) 反磁性体
( ) 室温励起子　　　( ) 永久磁石　　　( ) 要領
( ) 空格子点対　　　( ) 励起状態　　　( ) 消衰係数
( ) 励磁電流　　　　( ) 軽い正孔　　　( ) 地域
( ) 反磁場係数　　　( ) 反射係数　　　( ) 相空間

1. light hole
2. extinction coefficient
3. region, domain
4. region, zone
5. unit cell
6. vacancy pair
7. magnetizing current

8. gist, purport
9. transit time
10. diamagnet
11. permanent magnet
12. phase space
13. atomic form factor
14. electron orbit

13. reflectivity coefficient
14. photo-electron emission
15. intrinsic temperature region
16. demagnetization coefficient
17. room-temperature exciton
18. empty-lattice approximation
21. excitation conditions

Ex. 2.2 KANJI with the same ON reading

Here are some pairs of KANJI that share the same ON reading. Form meaningful JUKUGO, give the KANA transcriptions and translate.

1. (1)道　 (2)動　　　　運( )　　　　軌( )
2. (1)例　 (2)励　　　　比( )　　　　( )起
3. (1)引　 (2)因　　　　( )力　　　　原( )
4. (1)球　 (2)久　　　　( )面　　　　永( )
5. (1)相　 (2)走　　　　位( )　　　　( )行
6. (1)積　 (2)斥　　　　( )力　　　　面( )
7. (1)期　 (2)軌　　　　( )道　　　　周( )
8. (1)形　 (2)軽　　　　( )式　　　　( )孔

Ex. 2.3　Matching Japanese technical terms with definitions

Read each definition carefully, and then choose the appropriate technical term. Words that you have not yet encountered are listed following the definitions.

( )　引力	( )　斥力	( )　磁力
( )　永久	( )　励起	( )　軌道

1. 原子や分子が電磁放射や衝突によってエネルギーを与えられ、他の状態に上がる過程。
2. 同一種の電荷をもつ二物体間にはたらく力のように、両者間の距離を増やそうとする力。
3. 粒子や物体がその上を運動する閉じた道筋。
4. いつまでも続くこと。
5. 二つの物体が互いに引き合う力。
6. 磁石の磁極の間にはたらく力。

衝突	ショウトツ	collision	続く	つづく	to continue
電荷	デンカ	electric charge	引き合う	ひきあう	to mutually attract
両者の	リョウシャの	both	互いに	たがいに	mutually
距離	キョリ	distance	磁極	ジキョク	magnetic pole
閉じる	とじる	to close			

Ex. 2.4　Sentence translations

Read each sentence aloud several times and then translate it. You will encounter some KANJI that you do not yet know, but the words using these KANJI are listed following the sentences.

1. 原子核の磁気モーメントは核常磁性を示す。
2. 負の磁化率をもつ物質は反磁性体とよばれる。
3. 電子で満たされた閉殻の原子では、スピンと軌道モーメントは0であり、満たされていない電子殻のときにこれらのモーメントが現れる。
4. 固有温度領域では半導体の電気的性質は結晶内の不純物によっては大した変化は受けない。
5. 材料設計の観点からはW.A. Harrisonらが提案した結合軌道モデルが直観的に極めて明解であり、重要なアプローチの方法になると考えられる。
6. ここではド・ハース-ファン・アルフェン効果を選ぶが、それは一様な磁場内での金属の性質を示す1/Bの特徴的な周期を非常によく示しているからである。

17

核常磁性	カクジョウ ジセイ	nuclear paramagnetism		設計	セッケイ	design
				観点	カンテン	viewpoint
磁化率	ジカリツ	magnetic susceptibility		提案する	テイアンする	to propose
				直観的	チョッカンテキ	intuitive
閉殻	ヘイカク	closed shell		極めて	きわめて	very, extremely
現れる	あらわれる	to appear		明解	メイカイ	lucid explanation
半導体	ハンドウタイ	semiconductor		効果	コウカ	effect
大した	タイした	greatly, significantly		選ぶ	えらぶ	to choose
受ける	うける	to receive		一様な	イチヨウな	uniform
材料	ザイリョウ	material		非常に	ヒジョウに	extremely

Ex. 2.5 Paragraph translations

Read each paragraph aloud several times and then translate it. You will encounter some KANJI that you do not yet know, but the words using these KANJI are listed following the paragraphs.

1．磁気は量子力学とは不可分の関係にある。熱平衡における厳密な意味での古典力学系には、たとえ磁場があっても磁気が現れない。自由原子の磁気モーメントの起因には次の三つがある。電子に付与されたスピン、原子核をめぐる電子の軌道角運動量、および磁場が作用したときに誘起される軌道モーメントの変化分がこれである。

2．フェルミ面を決定するための強力な実験的手段がいくつか開発されている。その方法は磁気抵抗、異常表皮効果、サイクロトロン共鳴、磁気音響効果、シュブニコフ－ド・ハース効果、ド・ハース－ファン・アルフェン効果を含んでいる。電子の運動量分布に関する情報は陽電子消滅、コンプトン散乱、コーン効果からも得られる。

3．整数量子ホール効果(IQHE)および分数量子ホール効果(FQHE)は、最近の物理学において発見されたもっとも特筆すべき2つの物理現象である。多くの点において、二つの現象は非常に類似した基礎にある物理的特性と概念を分かち合う。たとえば、系の2次元性、縦抵抗の同時消滅をともなうh/e^2の単位でのホール抵抗の量子化、それから広がった状態の存在を引き起こす不規則性と磁場の間の競演などである。他の点では、両者はまったく異なった物理的原理と考え方を包含する。とくに、IQHEは垂直な強磁場の存在下での相互作用のない荷電粒子系の輸送特性の発見であると信じられている。これに反して、FQHEは多体系の基底状態の新しい形を生ずる粒子間の反発的相互作用から起こる。そのうえ、可動性(非局在)の素励起は分数電荷を有し、基底状態から上に有限のエネルギーをもって存在しなければならない。これらの分数電荷を有する励起はフェルミでもなくまたボーズ－アインシュタインでもない異常な統計に従うと考えられる。

不可分	フカブン	inseparable	現象	ゲンショウ	phenomenon
厳密な	ゲンミツな	strict, close	類似する	ルイジする	to resemble, be similar to
意味	イミ	meaning			
古典	コテン	classical	基礎	キソ	foundation, basis
たとえ		even if	特性	トクセイ	characteristic
自由	ジユウ	free	概念	ガイネン	concept
三つ	みっつ	three	分かち合う	わかちあう	to share
付与する	フヨする	to grant, give	縦-	たて-	longitudinal, vertical
めぐる		to move around			
角-	カク-	angular	広がる	ひろがる	to spread out, widen
誘起する	ユウキする	to induce			
手段	シュダン	means	存在	ソンザイ	existence
開発する	カイハツする	to develop	競演	キョウエン	competition
抵抗	テイコウ	resistance	包含する	ホウガンする	to include, imply
異常	イジョウ	anomalous, unusual, extraordinary	垂直な	スイチョクな	perpendicular
			荷電	カデン	charged
			輸送	ユソウ	transport
表皮	ヒョウヒ	skin	信じる	シンじる	to believe in
共鳴	キョウメイ	resonance	基底状態	キテイジョウタイ	ground state
音響	オンキョウ	acoustic			
分布	ブンプ	distribution	新しい	あたらしい	new
情報	ジョウホウ	information	可動性	カドウセイ	movable, mobile
消滅	ショウメツ	annihilation	非局在	ヒキョクザイ	non-localization
散乱	サンラン	scattering	有限の	ユウゲンの	finite
特筆	トクヒツ	noteworthy	統計	トウケイ	statistics

Translations for Ex. 2.4

1. The magnetic moment of the atomic nucleus exhibits nuclear paramagnetism.
2. Substances which have a negative magnetization are called diamagnets.
3. In atoms that have closed shells, which are filled with electrons, the spin and orbital moments are zero; when electron shells are not filled, these moments appear.
4. In the intrinsic temperature range, the electrical properties of semiconductors are not significantly changed by impurities within the crystal.
5. From the viewpoint of material design, the bond orbital model proposed by W.A. Harrison *et al.*, is intuitively very clear, and is expected to become an important method of approaching the problem.
6. Here we select the de Haas-van Alphen effect because it shows extremely well the 1/B characteristic period exhibited by a metal in a uniform magnetic field.

Translations for Ex. 2.5

1. Magnetism has an inseparable connection with quantum mechanics. For a strictly classical mechanical system in thermal equilibrium, there is no appearance of magnetism even in a magnetic field. The magnetic moment of a free atom has the following three causes. These are the spin contributed by the electrons, the orbital angular momentum of the electrons encircling the atomic nucleus, and the variable part of the orbital moment induced when interacting with a magnetic field.

2. Numerous powerful experimental techniques have been developed to determine the Fermi surface. Those methods include magnetoresistance, anomalous skin effect, cyclotron resonance, magnetoacoustic effect, Schubnikow-de Haas effect, and de Haas-van Alphen effect. Information related to the electron momentum distribution can also be obtained from positron annihilation, Compton scattering, and the Kohn effect.

3. The integral quantum Hall effect (IQHE) and the fractional quantum Hall effect (FQHE) are the physical phenomena most worthy of mention in modern physics. In many aspects, these two phenomena share extremely similar fundamental physical characteristics and concepts. Examples of these are the two-dimensionality of their systems, the quantization of their Hall resistances in units of h/e^2 at the same time as the disappearance of their longitudinal resistance, the competition between the magnetic field and irregularities that give rise to the existence of broadened states, and so forth. In other aspects, these two effects contain completely different physical principles and perspectives. In particular, in the IQHE it is believed that, in the presence of a strong perpendicular magnetic field, the transport characteristics for a non-interacting charged particle system have been discovered. In contrast, the FQHE produces a new form of many-body ground state in which repulsive interactions occur between the particles. Moreover, the mobile (non-localized) elementary excitations have fractional electric charge, and they must have a finite energy to rise above the ground state. These excitations which have fractional electric charge are thought to obey an unusual statistics that is neither Fermi nor Bose-Einstein.

荷	カ	load
	に	load

陥	カン	caving in, cavitation
	おちい (る)	to fall into {xu-verb}

具	グ	tool

欠	ケツ	lacking; absent; defect
	か (く)	to lack, fail in

弾	ダン	bullet; rebound

張	チョウ	stretching
	は (る)	to stretch

排	ハイ	expelling

頻	ヒン	repetitive

幅	フク	width
	はば	width

由	ユ; ユウ	reason; intention

荷 陥
具 欠
弾 張
排 頻
幅 由

荷

陰電荷	インデンカ	negative charge
間欠荷重	カンケツカジュウ	intermittent load
空間電荷	クウカンデンカ	space charge
電荷	デンカ	electric charge
陽電荷	ヨウデンカ	positive charge

陥

欠陥	ケッカン	defect
格子欠陥	コウシケッカン	lattice defect
フレンケル欠陥	フレンケルケッカン	Frenkel defect

具

金具	かなグ	metal fitting, bracket
器具	キグ	appliance, tool, apparatus
具体的な	グタイテキな	concrete, definite
工具	コウグ	tool
道具	ドウグ	tool

欠

点欠格	テンケッカク	point defect
間欠荷重	カンケツカジュウ	intermittent load
欠陥	ケッカン	defect
欠点	ケッテン	defect
格子欠陥	コウシケッカン	lattice defect
フレンケル欠陥	フレンケルケッカン	Frenkel defect

弾

強弾性	キョウダンセイ	ferroelasticity
磁気弾性結合	ジキダンセイケツゴウ	magnetoelastic bonding
弾性エネルギー	ダンセイエネルギー	elastic energy
螺旋の弾性エネルギー	ラセンのダンセイエネルギー	helical elastic energy

張

張力	チョウリョク	tension
引張り応力	ひっぱりオウリョク	tensile stress

排

パウリの排他原理	パウリのハイタゲンリ	Pauli exclusion principle

頻

飛び移り頻度	とびうつりヒンド	hopping frequency
頻度	ヒンド	frequency

幅

井戸の幅	いどのはば	(potential) well width
振幅変調	シンプクヘンチョウ	amplitude modulation
増幅器	ゾウフクキ	amplifier
発光スペクトル幅	ハッコウスペクトルはば	optical emission spectral width
負質量増幅器	フシツリョウゾウフクキ	negative mass amplifier
ブロッホ振動振幅	ブロッホシンドウシンプク	Bloch oscillation amplitude

由

三次元自由電子	サンジゲンジユウデンシ	three-dimensional free electron
自由	ジユウ	freedom
自由電子	ジユウデンシ	free electron
自由電子エネルギー	ジユウデンシエネルギー	free electron energy
自由電子気体	ジユウデンシキタイ	free electron gas
自由電子フェルミ気体	ジユウデンシフェルミキタイ	free electron Fermi gas
自由電子モデル	ジユウデンシモデル	free electron model
自由度	ジユウド	degree of freedom
ヘルムホルツの自由 　エネルギー	ヘルムホルツのジユウ 　エネルギー	Helmholtz free energy
有機自由基	ユウキジユウキ	organic free radical
理由	リユウ	reason, cause

SUPPLEMENTARY VOCABULARY USING DEDICATED KANJI PAIRS

The KANJI that form these pairs will rarely be seen separately in solid-state physics material. They are more easily remembered as pairs.

幾何	キカ	geometric
幾何学的構造因子	キカガクテキコウゾウインシ	geometrical structure factor
幾何学	キカガク	geometry

| 螺旋 | ラセン | helix |
| 螺旋の弾性エネルギー | ラセンのダンセイエネルギー | helical elastic energy |

SUPPLEMENTARY VOCABULARY USING KANJI FROM CHAPTER 13

イルメナイト構造	イルメナイトコウゾウ	ilmenite structure
基礎方程式	キソホウテイシキ	fundamental equation
極値をもつ軌道	キョクチをもつキドウ	extremal orbit
高純度ヘテロ構造 FET	コウジュンドヘテロコウゾウ FET	high-purity heterostructure FET
鎖状構造	サジョウコウゾウ	chain structure
サブバンド構造	サブバンドコウゾウ	sub-band structure
受領	ジュリョウ	receipt, acceptance
正常過程	セイジョウカテイ	direct process
速度変調トランジスター	ソクドヘンチョウトランジスター	velocity-modulation transistor
ペロブスカイト構造	ペロブスカイトコウゾウ	perovskite structure
量子マイクロヘテロ 構造	リョウシマイクロヘテロ コウゾウ	quantum micro-heterostructure

EXERCISES

Ex. 3.1 Matching Japanese and English terms

( ) 頻度   ( ) 幾何学   ( ) 引張り応力
( ) 強弾性   ( ) 自由度   ( ) 磁気弾性結合
( ) 理由   ( ) 間欠荷重   ( ) 有機自由基
( ) 鎖状構造   ( ) 正常過程   ( ) 基礎方程式
( ) 増幅器   ( ) 陰電荷   ( ) 振幅変調
( ) 螺旋   ( ) 速度変調   ( ) 自由電子
( ) 陽電荷   ( ) 具体的   ( ) 格子欠陥

1. amplifier   8. frequency   15. tensile stress
2. chain structure   9. direct process   16. ferroelasticity
3. velocity modulation   10. positive charge   17. concrete, definite
4. lattice defect   11. geometry   18. negative charge
5. amplitude modulation   12. free electron   19. organic free radical
6. reason, cause   13. degree of freedom   20. magnetoelastic coupling
7. intermittent load   14. helix   21. fundamental equation

Ex. 3.2 KANJI with the same ON reading

Here are some pairs of KANJI that share the same ON reading. Form meaningful JUKUGO, give the KANA transcriptions and translate.

1. (1)欠   (2)結   ( )合   ( )陥
2. (1)長   (2)張   成( )   ( )力
3. (1)有   (2)由   ( )無   自( )
4. (1)荷   (2)何   幾( )   電( )
5. (1)基   (2)幾   ( )質   ( )何
6. (1)陥   (2)間   欠( )   空( )
7. (1)線   (2)旋   螺( )   流( )

25

Ex. 3.3　Matching Japanese technical terms with definitions

（　）飛び移り頻度　　　　　（　）鎖状構造　　　　　（　）振幅変調
（　）欠点　　　　　　　　　（　）強弾性　　　　　　（　）自由電子

1. 原子が単位時間に ν 回障壁を通過しようとするが、その各々の試みにおける成功の確率。
2. ある結晶が機械的応力のないときに、方向に関して二つまたはそれ以上の安定状態をもち、さらに機械的応力を加えることにより、一方の安定状態から他の状態へと可逆的に移しうる場合、その結晶の弾性特性。
3. 原子が鎖のように並んでいる配置。
4. 特定の原子内に拘束されていない電子。
5. 波の振幅が伝送される情報に従って変化する変調。
6. 結晶の構造の不規則の場所。

障壁	ショウヘキ	barrier	鎖	くさり	chain
各々の	おのおのの	individual, each	並ぶ	ならぶ	to be lined up
試み	こころみ	attempt, test	配置	ハイチ	arrangement
成功	セイコウ	success	特定	トクテイ	specific, particular
確率	カクリツ	probability	拘束する	コウソクする	to restrain,
機械的	キカイテキ	mechanical			constrain
安定	アンテイ	stable	波	なみ	wave
可逆的に	カギャクテキに	reversibly	伝送する	デンソウする	to transmit

(*Note*: Do not confuse 確率 with 確立, which is also read カクリツ, but means "establishing.")

Ex. 3.4　Sentence translations

1. 図には一様および変調ドーピングの場合のドナー不純物の準位および不純物を導入したことによる空間電荷の影響によって、バンド端が曲率をもつ様子が示されている。
2. 量子井戸や超格子で準2次元電子系を作るためには、不純物をドープする必要がある。
3. 井戸の中の電子は、井戸に垂直な面内では自由電子として振る舞うが、井戸に沿う方向にはポテンシャル障壁があって電子は井戸付近に局在し、波動関数は指数関数的に減少する。

準位	ジュンイ	(energy) level	振る舞う	ふるまう	to behave
導入する	ドウニュウする	to introduce	沿う	そう	to follow along
影響	エイキョウ	influence	付近	フキン	neighborhood,
-端	-タン	edge			vicinity
曲率	キョクリツ	curvature	波動関数	ハドウカンスウ	wave function
準	ジュン	quasi-	減少する	ゲンショウする	to decrease

Ex. 3.5   Paragraph translations

1. 固体の重要な特性のあるものは、母体結晶の性質によってと同様、不完全性によっても制御される。その際母体結晶は不完全性に対する単なる入れ物、溶媒、ないしは、母体としてふるまっているにすぎないこともある。ある半導体の電気伝導率は化学的不純物のわずかな量によってほとんど定まる。多くの結晶の色とルミネッセンスは不純物か不完全性によって生ずる。原子の拡散は不純物や不完全性により多いに促進されることがある。機械的および塑性的性質は一般に不完全性により制御される。

2. 最も簡単な不完全性は空格子点で、これは格子点から原子またはイオンが失われたもので、ショットキー欠陥として知られている。原子を内部の格子点から結晶の表面上の格子点に移すことによって完全結晶内にショットキー欠陥をつくることができる。空格子点の他の形にフレンケル欠陥がある。これは原子が格子点から格子間位置、すなわち、正規には原子によって占められていない位置に移されたものである。純粋なアルカリハライド結晶の中で最も普通の空格子点はショットキー欠陥である。また銀ハライドでの最も普通の空格子はフレンケル欠陥である。

3. アルカリおよび銀のハライドの結晶の電気伝導の機構は普通はイオンの運動であり、電子のそれではない。このことは運ばれた電荷と質量とを比較することにより確認されてきた。後者は結晶に接している電極の一方の上に析出した物質から測定される。

母体	ボタイ	host body	一般に	イッパンに	generally
同様	ドウヨウ	same, similarity	失う	うしなう	to lose
完全性	カンゼンセイ	perfection	占める	しめる	to occupy
制御する	セイギョする	to control, govern	純粋	ジュンスイ	purity
際	サイ	occasion	普通	フツウ	usual, ordinary
単なる	タンなる	simple	比較する	ヒカクする	to compare
溶媒	ヨウバイ	solvent	確認する	カクニンする	to confirm
伝導率	デンドウリツ	conductivity	後者	コウシャ	the latter
拡散	カクサン	diffusion	接する	セッする	to contact
促進する	ソクシンする	to promote	析出する	セキシュツする	to deposit
塑性的	ソセイテキ	plastic			

Translations for Ex. 3.4

1. Shown in the figure is the appearance of band-edge curvature caused by the effect of space charges from impurity levels of uniform and modulation-doped donor impurities as well as from introduced impurities.
2. It is necessary to dope with impurities in order to form the quasi-two-dimensional electron system in quantum wells and superlattices.
3. The electrons in the well move around as free electrons within the perpendicular well walls. Along the direction of the well, they are localized in the vicinity of the well by the potential barriers and have wave functions that decrease exponentially.

Translations for Ex. 3.5

1. Some important characterics of solids are controlled by imperfections as well as by the properties of the host crystal. In those cases, the host crystal sometimes behaves as nothing more than a host body—a solvent or a receptacle for the imperfections. The electronic conductivity of certain semiconductors is almost completely determined by minute quantities of chemical impurities. The colors and luminescence of many crystals are produced by impurities or imperfections. There are cases where atomic diffusion is greatly promoted by impurities and imperfections. Mechanical and plastic properties are generally governed by imperfections.

2. The simplest imperfection, known as a Schottky defect, is an empty lattice point where an atom or ion is absent from a lattice point. A Schottky defect can be created in a perfect crystal when an atom is moved from an interior lattice site to a lattice site on the crystal surface. Another form of empty lattice site (vacancy) is called a Frenkel defect. Here an atom moves from a lattice point to an interstitial position, i.e., a position normally not occupied by atoms. The most common vacancies found in pure alkali-halide crystals are Schottky defects, while the most common vacancies found in silver halides are Frenkel defects.

3. The mechanism for electrical conduction in alkali and silver halide crystals is usually the movement of ions, not that of electrons. This is confirmed by the comparison of transported electric charge and mass. The latter can measured using the material deposited on an electrode contacting the crystal.

却	キャク	(doing) completely
鏡	キョウ かがみ	mirror mirror
顕	ケン	disclosing, appearing
査	サ	investigating
障	ショウ	hinder; harm
選	セン えら (ぶ)	selecting to select, choose
択	タク	selecting
壁	ヘキ かべ	wall wall
冷	レイ ひ (やす) ひ (える)	cold, cool to cool, refrigerate to grow cold, cool off
零	レイ	zero

却　鏡
顕　査
障　選
択　壁
冷　零

却

エントロピー不変消磁法による冷却	エントロピーフヘンショウジホウによるレイキャク	refrigeration by adiabatic demagnetization
冷却器	レイキャクキ	cooler

鏡

鏡像	キョウゾウ	mirror image
鏡像力	キョウゾウリョク	image force
鏡面反射	キョウメンハンシャ	mirror reflection
光学顕微鏡	コウガクケンビキョウ	optical microscope
走査トンネル電子顕微鏡	ソウサトンネルデンシケンビキョウ	scanning tunneling electron microscope (STEM)
対物鏡	タイブツキョウ	objective lens
電子顕微鏡	デンシケンビキョウ	electron microscope
平面鏡	ヘイメンキョウ	plane mirror

顕

光学顕微鏡	コウガクケンビキョウ	optical microscope
走査トンネル電子顕微鏡	ソウサトンネルデンシケンビキョウ	scanning tunneling electron microscope (STEM)
電子顕微鏡	デンシケンビキョウ	electron microscope

査

走査	ソウサ	scanning
走査トンネル電子顕微鏡	ソウサトンネルデンシケンビキョウ	scanning tunneling electron microscope (STEM)
調査中	チョウサチュウ	under investigation

障

障壁	ショウヘキ	barrier
障壁の幅	ショウヘキのはば	barrier width
ショットキー障壁	ショットキーショウヘキ	Schottky barrier
トンネル障壁	トンネルショウヘキ	tunnel barrier
ヘテロ障壁	ヘテロショウヘキ	hetero-barrier
ポテンシャル障壁	ポテンシャルショウヘキ	potential barrier

選

k-選択率	k-センタクリツ	k-selectivity
選択	センタク	selection
選択性	センタクセイ	selectivity
選択則	センタクソク	selection rule
選択ドープ	センタクドープ	selective doping

択

k-選択率	k-センタクリツ	k-selectivity
選択	センタク	selection
選択性	センタクセイ	selectivity
選択則	センタクソク	selection rule
選択ドープ	センタクドープ	selective doping

壁

外壁	ガイヘキ	outside wall
障壁	ショウヘキ	barrier
障壁の幅	ショウヘキのはば	barrier width
ショットキー障壁	ショットキーショウヘキ	Schottky barrier
トンネル障壁	トンネルショウヘキ	tunnel barrier
ネール磁壁	ネールジヘキ	Neel magnetic wall
ブロッホ磁壁	ブロッホジヘキ	Bloch magnetic wall
ヘテロ障壁	ヘテロショウヘキ	hetero-barrier
ポテンシャル障壁	ポテンシャルショウヘキ	potential barrier

冷

エントロピー不変消磁 法による冷却	エントロピイフヘンショウジ ホウによるレイキャク	refrigeration by adiabatic demagnetization
冷却器	レイキャクキ	cooler

零

絶対零度	ゼッタイレイド	absolute zero
零点	レイテン	zero point
零点運動	レイテンウンドウ	zero-point motion
零点エネルギー	レイテンエネルギー	zero-point energy
零点振動	レイテンシンドウ	zero-point oscillation
零点補正	レイテンホセイ	zero-point correction

荷重曲線	カジュウキョクセン	load curve
最近接原子間	サイキンセツゲンシカン	nearest-atom spacing
ジョゼフソン接合	ジョゼフソンセツゴウ	Josephson junction
接合レーザー	セツゴウレーザー	junction laser
接合領域	セツゴウリョウイキ	junction region
単一ヘテロ接合	タンイツヘテロセツゴウ	single heterojunction
ニュートンの運動の 第2法則	ニュートンのウンドウの ダイ2ホウソク	Newton's second law of motion
微細構造定数	ビサイコウゾウテイスウ	fine-structure constant
微弱な	ビジャクな	feeble
ヘテロ接合	ヘテロセツゴウ	heterojunction
約数	ヤクスウ	divisor {math}
類似	ルイジ	similarity, resemblance
類推する	ルイスイする	to analogize
六方空間格子	ロッポウクウカンコウシ	hexagonal space lattice

EXERCISES

Ex. 4.1 Matching Japanese and English terms

( ) 外壁   ( ) 鏡面反射   ( ) 最近接原子間
( ) 類似   ( ) 零点補正   ( ) 微細構造定数
( ) 冷却器   ( ) 荷重曲線   ( ) 電子顕微鏡
( ) 走査   ( ) 調査中   ( ) 六方空間格子
( ) 類推   ( ) 微弱な   ( ) 光学顕微鏡
( ) 障壁   ( ) 対物鏡   ( ) 零点運動
( ) 平面鏡   ( ) 選択則   ( ) 零点振動
( ) 選択率   ( ) 鏡像力   ( ) 接合領域

1. zero-point oscillation   9. junction region   17. cooler
2. outside wall   10. mirror reflection   18. zero-point correction
3. electron microscope   11. fine-structure constant   19. scanning
4. under investigation   12. hexagonal space lattice   20. nearest-atom spacing
5. load curve   13. similarity   21. feeble
6. optical microscope   14. zero-point motion   22. analogy
7. plane mirror   15. selection rule   23. selectivity
8. barrier   16. objective lens   24. image force

Ex. 4.2 KANJI with the same ON reading

Here are some pairs of KANJI that share the same ON reading. Form meaningful JUKUGO, give the KANA transcriptions and translate.

1. (1)鏡   (2)強   ( )像   ( )度
2. (1)験   (2)顕   ( )微鏡   実( )
3. (1)障   (2)消   ( )壁   ( )磁
4. (1)選   (2)線   曲( )   ( )択
5. (1)零   (2)冷   ( )却   ( )点

Ex. 4.3 Section headings from solid-state physics books
Read these section headings aloud several times and translate them.

1. 光学的過程と励起子
2. モット・ワニエ励起子
3. 点欠陥
4. 同位体効果
5. 電子分極率
6. ソフト光学フォノン
7. 光学セラミックス
8. 空格子点
9. 色中心
10. 磁気バブル磁区
11. 非晶質固体
12. 運動方程式
13. p-n接合
14. クラマース・クローニッヒの関係式
15. 常磁性塩のエントロピー不変消磁法による冷却
16. 結晶中のラマン効果
17. X線光電子分光法
18. BCS基準状態
19. ピエゾ電気
20. アモルファス強磁性磁石
21. メーザー作用の原理
22. 伝導電子の常磁性磁化率
23. ガラス状シリカの構造
24. 単原子アモルファス物質
25. ガラス状シリカの構造
26. 分数量子ホール効果

Ex. 4.4 Choosing the correct KANJI

Here are some pairs of KANJI that are somewhat similar in appearance or that have a common radical. Form meaningful JUKUGO (as in Ex. 1.2), give the KANA transcriptions and translate.

1.	(1)負	(2)具	金( )	( )電荷
2.	(1)道	(2)導	( )具	伝( )
3.	(1)水	(2)永	( )久	( )素
4.	(1)個	(2)固	( )体	三( )
5.	(1)周	(2)調	( )期	変( )
6.	(1)径	(2)軽	半( )	( )孔
7.	(1)幾	(2)機	( )構	( )何
8.	(1)成	(2)域	領( )	( )長
9.	(1)状	(2)伏	降( )	形( )
10.	(1)何	(2)荷	幾( )	( )重
11.	(1)久	(2)欠	( )点	永( )
12.	(1)欠	(2)次	( )陥	( )元
13.	(1)領	(2)頻	( )度	要( )
14.	(1)各	(2)格	( )部	規( )

Ex. 4.5   Sentence translations

1. p-n接合は二つの領域に分けられた一つの単結晶からできている。
2. 照射されている接合に現れる順電圧は光起電力効果とよばれる。
3. 拡散により少量の電荷が移動するために、p側には余分の(-)にイオン化したアクセプター原子が残され、n側には余分の(+)にイオン化されたドナー原子が残される。
4. 逆バイアス電圧の場合には、負の電圧がp領域にかかり、正の電圧がn領域にかかるので、二つの領域間のポテンシャルの差が増加する。

照射する	ショウシャする	to irradiate	残す	のこす	to leave behind
順	ジュン	forward (bias)	逆	ギャク	inverse, reverse
-側	-がわ	side	差	サ	difference
余分	ヨブン	extra, excess			

Ex. 4.6   Paragraph translations

1. 1Kよりずっと低い温度をつくる最初の方法はエントロピー不変消磁、すなわち断熱消磁の方法である。この方法によって0.001Kから、さらに低い温度に到達している。この方法は、ある一定の温度における磁気モーメントの系のエントロピーが、磁場を作用させると低下するという原理に基づいている。

2. 図には、3次元走査トンネル電子顕微鏡写真として知られる高感度撮影法による顕微鏡像を示す。この写真はシリコン表面の2次元走査等高線から構造されたものである。2個の菱面形の単位格子が見られ、その長い方の対角線の長さは4.6nmである。単位格子内の丘や谷は垂直方向に0.28nmの凸凹をもっている。

3. これまでに明らかにされたガリウム砒素 - アルミニウム・ガリウム砒素ポテンシャル井戸構造、超格子構造の光学的特性の中には新しい光デバイスへの応用の可能性を示唆するものが多く、実際にデバイスを目指した研究も活発におこなわれている。例えば、量子サイズ効果によって生じる高い状態密度をもつ量子準位間の量子転移を利用する量子井戸構造半導体レーザー、室温でも安定に存在する2次元励起子を利用した雪崩増倍形光検出器、およびドーピング超格子を利用した波長可変発光ダイオードなどを挙げることができる。しかしながら現時点では量子井戸構造半導体レーザーを除いては、新しいデバイスとしての可能性が十分に確認されているものはない。したがって以下では、量子井戸構造半導体レーザーの特徴、問題点、今後の展望等を中心に記述する。量子井戸構造半導体レーザーを単に量子井戸レーザーと略記する。

低い	ひくい	low	密度	ミツド	density
最初の	サイショの	first	利用する	リヨウする	to utilize, make use of
到達する	トウタツする	to attain, reach	室温	シツオン	room temperature
低下する	テイカする	to fall, drop	雪崩	なだれ	avalanche
写真	シャシン	photograph	検出器	ケンシュツキ	detector
感度	カンド	sensitivity	波長可変	ハチョウ カヘン	variable wavelength
撮影	サツエイ	photography	挙げる	あげる	to mention, cite
像	ゾウ	image	現時点	ゲンジテン	at this time
菱面形	リョウメン ケイ	rhombohedral	除く	のぞく	to omit, remove
丘	おか	hill	問題	モンダイ	problem
谷	たに	valley	今後	コンゴ	from now on
凸凹	でこぼこ	unevenness	展望	テンボウ	view
可能性	カノウセイ	possibility	記述する	キジュツする	to describe
示唆する	シサする	to suggest	略記する	リャッキする	to outline, sketch briefly
実際に	ジッサイに	actually, in reality			
研究	ケンキュウ	research			
活発	カッパツ	active, lively			

Translations for Ex. 4.5

1. A p-n junction is made from a single crystal divided into two regions.
2. The forward voltage that appears in an illuminated junction is called the photovoltaic effect.
3. Because small amounts of electric charge move by diffusion, the ionized acceptor atoms on the p side end up with an excess of negative charges and the ionized donor atoms on the n side end up with an excess of positive charges.
4. Under a reverse bias voltage, the negative voltage is applied to the p-region and the positive voltage is applied to the n-region. Therefore, the potential difference between the two regions increases.

Translations for Ex. 4.6

1. The first method for making temperatures well below 1 K is that of constant entropy demagnetization, namely, the adiabatic demagnetization method. By this method temperatures below even 0.001 K are attained. It is based on the principle that for a fixed temperature the entropy of a magnetic moment system can be reduced by the action of a magnetic field.

2. The figure shows a microscopic image made using a high-sensitivity imaging method known as 3-dimensional scanning tunnelling electron microscope photography. This picture is constructed from 2-dimensional scan contour lines of a silicon surface. Two rhombohedral unit lattices can be seen which have diagonals measuring 4.6 nm in length. Hills and valleys within these unit cells have an unevenness of 0.28 nm in the perpendicular direction.

3. We have, up to this point, made numerous suggestions regarding the possibilities of applications for the optical characteristics of gallium-arsenide/aluminum-gallium-arsenide quantum wells and superlattice structures to new optical devices. Research aimed at actually developing such devices is being actively carried out. For example, we can mention semiconductor lasers using quantum well structures that utilize transitions between quantum levels that have the high density of states produced by the quantum size effect, avalanche photo-multiplier detectors that use 2-dimensional excitons that exist in a stable form even at room temperature, as well as variable-wavelength light-emitting diodes, and so on, which use doped superlattices. However, at the present time, with the exception of the quantum-well structure semiconductor laser, the possibilities of these new devices are not adequately demonstrated. Thus in the following, we will center our description on such topics as the characteristics, problem areas, and prospects for quantum well structure semiconductor lasers. We will abbreviate quantum-well structure semiconductor lasers as simply quantum well lasers.

縁	エン	connection; relation
擬	ギ	pseudo- ; imitation
凝	ギョウ	freezing; congealing
均	キン	average; equal
失	シツ うしな (う)	loss to lose
絶	ゼツ た (えず)	cessation; extremity ceaselessly
損	ソン そこ (なう)	loss, damage to harm, injure
答	トウ こた (え) こた (える)	answer answer to answer, respond
様	ヨウ さま	appearance; state situation; condition
歪	ひず (み)	strain; distortion

縁　擬

凝　均

失　絶

損　答

様　歪

縁

絶縁	ゼツエン	insulation
絶縁体	ゼツエンタイ	insulator

擬

擬ポテンシャル	ギポテンシャル	pseudopotential
擬ポテンシャル法	ギポテンシャルホウ	pseudopotential method
第1原理の	ダイイチゲンリの	first principle
擬ポテンシャル	ギポテンシャル	pseudopotential

凝

凝固	ギョウコ	solidification, coagulation
凝集エネルギー	ギョウシュウエネルギー	cohesive energy

均

場の平均値	ばのヘイキンチ	average field value
平均	ヘイキン	average (value)
平均磁場近似	ヘイキンジばキンジ	mean-field approximation
平均自由行程	ヘイキンジユウコウテイ	mean free path

失

エネルギー損失関数	エネルギーソンシツカンスウ	energy loss function
高速粒子のエネルギー	コウソクリュウシのエネルギー	energy loss of
損失	ソンシツ	high-energy particles
消失	ショウシツ	disappearance

絶

絶縁	ゼツエン	insulation
絶縁体	ゼツエンタイ	insulator
絶対-	ゼッタイ-	absolute, unconditional

損

エネルギー損失関数	エネルギーソンシツカンスウ	energy loss function
高速粒子のエネルギー	コウソクリュウシのエネルギー	energy loss of
損失	ソンシツ	high-energy particles
損害	ソンガイ	damage
破損	ハソン	damage, breakage

答

応答関数	オウトウカンスウ	response function
複素応答関数	フクソオウトウカンスウ	complex response function

様

一様ドーピング	イチヨウドーピング	uniform doping
一様モード	イチヨウモード	uniform mode
様々な	さまざまな	various
同様の	ドウヨウの	similar; same kind, same way

歪

磁気歪み	ジキひずみ	magnetic strain
ピエゾ電気歪み定数	ピエゾデンキひずみテイスウ	piezoelectric strain constant
歪み硬化	ひずみコウカ	strain hardening

SUPPLEMENTARY VOCABULARY USING KANJI FROM CHAPTER 15

最小金属的伝導率	サイショウキンゾクテキ デンドウリツ	smallest metallic conductivity
ショットキー異常	ショットキーイジョウ	Schottky anomaly
鉄族イオン	テツゾクイオン	iron group ion
配置比熱	ハイチヒネツ	configurational heat capacity
立方硫化亜鉛構造	リッポウリュウカアエンコウゾウ	cubic zinc sulfide structure

EXERCISES

Ex. 5.1 Matching Japanese and English terms

( ) 凝固　　　　　( ) 配置比熱　　　　　( ) ショットキー異常
( ) 同様の　　　　( ) 鉄族イオン　　　　( ) 擬ポテンシャル法
( ) 様々な　　　　( ) 磁気歪み　　　　　( ) ピエゾ電気歪み定数
( ) 損害　　　　　( ) 平均自由行程　　　( ) 立方硫化亜鉛構造
( ) 歪み硬化　　　( ) 場の平均値　　　　( ) 凝集エネルギー
( ) 絶縁　　　　　( ) 平均磁場近似　　　( ) エネルギー損失関数
( ) 破損　　　　　( ) 複素応答関数　　　( ) 一様ドーピング
( ) 絶縁体　　　　( ) 最小金属的伝導率

1. cohesive energy
2. damage
3. cubic zinc sulfide structure
4. Schottky anomaly
5. the same kind
6. strain hardening
7. pseudopotential method
8. mean free path
9. coagulation
10. complex response function
11. various
12. iron group ion
13. piezoelectric strain constant
14. damage, breakage
15. mean-field approximation
16. insulator
17. insulation
18. uniform doping
19. configurational heat capacity
20. smallest metallic conductivity
21. magnetic strain
22. average field value
23. energy loss function

Ex. 5.2 Choosing the correct KANJI

#	(1)	(2)			
1.	(1)線	(2)縁	絶( )		曲( )
2.	(1)擬	(2)凝	( )集		( )ポテンシャル
3.	(1)均	(2)約	平( )		( )数
4.	(1)走	(2)失	損( )		( )査
5.	(1)結	(2)絶	( )合		( )縁
6.	(1)損	(2)指	( )数		( )失
7.	(1)答	(2)管	応( )		( )状
8.	(1)構	(2)様	( )成		一( )
9.	(1)歪	(2)空	( )気		( )み
10.	(1)約	(2)的	( )数		目( )

Ex. 5.3   Sentence translations

1. 結晶性物質の強度は塑性変形によって増加する。このことを加工硬化あるいは歪み硬化という。

2. 青木・近藤が述べているように、各々のランダウ準位内に非局在状態が存在しなければ、それぞれのランダウ準位はホール電流を運ぶことはできない。

3. 分子線源は蒸発用原料を入れるクルーシブルと、加熱するためのヒーターおよびシャッターからできている。

4. 低電界領域における、選択ドープGaAs/n-AlGaAsヘテロ構造のヘテロ界面に平行な方向の電子移動度と電子濃度(面濃度)は通常のホール測定によって容易に得られる。

加工硬化	カコウコウカ	work hardening	原料	ゲンリョウ	source material
青木	あおき	Aoki {surname}	電界	デンカイ	electric field
近藤	コンドウ	Kondo {surname}	界面	カイメン	interface
分子線	ブンシセン	molecular beam	濃度	ノウド	concentration, density
-源	-ゲン	source	容易に	ヨウイに	often, well

(*Note*: 原, meaning "source," is used more abstractly than 源, which originally meant "water spring.")

Ex. 5.4   Paragraph translation

　　量子マイクロヘテロ構造には、電子の波動性のために様々な新しい性質が現われる。それらを大別すると、1:量子サイズ効果による電子および正孔の閉じ込めにより、2次元電子状態が形成されることによる効果、2:閉じ込められた電子とドナーあるいは正孔とが空間的に分離されるために生じる効果、3:電子のトンネル効果や干渉効果に従う各種の非線形効果による効果などに分けることができる。さらに、急峻なヘテロ接合では、障壁の上から下(または下から上)に電子を加速(減速)することにより、ホットエレクトロンの流れを効率よく生成(または消滅)できるため、準古典的ではあるが、様々な新しい機能やデバイスを実現することができる。このように量子効果により新物性を作り出す一連の試みは、k空間の設計を主体とする従来のエネルギーバンド工学とは大きく異なって、実空間における波動関数や分布関数を設計し制御するという点で、半導体工学および半導体物理学の新分野を形成しているといえよう。

大別する	タイベツする	to classify broadly	実現する	ジツゲンする	to be realized
閉じ込め	とじこめ	confinement	一連の	イチレンの	a chain (series) of
分離する	ブンリする	to separate	設計	セッケイ	design, plan
干渉	カンショウ	interference	主体	シュタイ	main constituent
急峻な	キュウシュンな	abrupt	従来の	ジュウライの	conventional
減速する	ゲンソクする	deceleration	分布関数	ブンプ	distribution
効率	コウリツ	efficiency		カンスウ	function
機能	キノウ	function, capability	分野	ブンヤ	field (of study)

43

Translations for Ex. 5.3

1. The strength of crystalline matter increases with plastic deformation. This is called work hardening or strain hardening.
2. As stated by Aoki and Kondo, if extended (non-local) states do not exist within a particular Landau level, that Landau level will be unable to carry any Hall current.
3. A molecular beam source is made from a crucible loaded with evaporation source materials, a heater for adding heat, and a shutter.
4. In the low electric field region for selectively-doped GaAs/n-AlGaAs heterostructures, one can use ordinary Hall measurements to easily obtain the electron density (surface density) and the electron mobility parallel to the hetero-interface.

Translation for Ex. 5.4

Various new properties appear in quantum micro-heterostructures because of the wave-like nature of the electrons. They can be roughly divided into the following: 1) effects based on the formation of two-dimensional electron states and the confinement of electrons and holes via the quantum size effect; 2) effects produced by the spatial separation of electrons from donors and holes; and 3) effects that can be classified according to the kinds of non-linear effects originating from electron tunneling and interference. Also, it is possible to efficiently create (or annihilate) hot electron flow from the acceleration (or deceleration) of electrons as they climb up (or fall down) barriers in abrupt heterojunctions. Therefore, even though hot electrons exist semi-classically, it is possible to produce various new functions and devices. The series of experiments that produce new physical properties from these kinds of quantum effects is said to create new fields of semiconductor engineering and semiconductor physics based on the control and design of real-space wave functions and distribution functions. This is very different from conventional energy-band engineering, which primarily dealt with k-space design.

依	イ	depending (on); intact
	よ (る)	to depend (on)

横	オウ	transverse; horizontal
	よこ	transverse; horizontal

感	カン	feeling, sensation

緩	カン	relaxation, mitigation

局	キョク	local

軸	ジク	axis, axle

縦	ジュウ	longitudinal; vertical
	たて	longitudinal; vertical

親	シン	intimacy, closeness
	おや	parent

双	ソウ	a pair; a set

保	ホ	preserving, maintaining
	たも (つ)	to maintain, preserve

依　横
感　緩
局　軸
縦　親
双　保

45

依

依存性	イゾンセイ	dependence
温度依存性	オンドイゾンセイ	temperature dependence
成長温度依存性	セイチョウオンドイゾンセイ	growth temperature dependence
飽和磁化の温度依存性	ホウワジカのオンドイゾンセイ	temperature dependence of saturation magnetization

横

横緩和時間	よこカンワジカン	transverse relaxation time
横光学モード	よこコウガクモード	transverse optical mode
横光学フォノン	よこコウガクフォノン	transverse optical phonon

感

感光度	カンコウド	photosensitivity
感度	カンド	sensitivity
相対感受率	ソウタイカンジュリツ	relative permittivity

緩

緩和時間	カンワジカン	relaxation time
スピン・格子緩和時間	スピン・コウシカンワジカン	spin-lattice relaxation time
縦緩和時間	たてカンワジカン	longitudinal relaxation time
バンド内キャリヤ	バンドナイキャリヤ	intraband carrier
緩和現象	カンワゲンショウ	relaxation phenomenon
モード間緩和	モードカンカンワ	inter-mode relaxation
横緩和時間	よこカンワジカン	transverse relaxation time

局

アンダーソン局在	アンダーソンキョクザイ	Anderson localization
局在状態	キョクザイジョウタイ	localized state
局在長	キョクザイチョウ	localization length
局所電場	キョクショデンば	local (electric) field

軸

軸方向応力	ジクホウコウオウリョク	axial stress
主軸	シュジク	principal axis
短軸	タンジク	minor axis
長軸	チョウジク	major axis
同軸	ドウジク	coaxial

縦

縦緩和時間	たてカンワジカン	longitudinal relaxation time

親

第一電子親和度	ダイイチデンシシンワド	primary electron affinity
第二電子親和度	ダイニデンシシンワド	secondary electron affinity
電子親和力	デンシシンワリョク	electron affinity

双

磁気双極子	ジキソウキョクシ	magnetic dipole
双極子	ソウキョクシ	dipole
双極子分極率	ソウキョクシブンキョクリツ	dipolar polarizability
双極子モーメント	ソウキョクシモーメント	dipole moment
双曲線関数	ソウキョクセンカンスウ	hyperbolic function
双晶変形	ソウショウヘンケイ	twinning

保

確保する	カクホする	to secure
電子数保存	デンシスウホゾン	conservation of electron number
保持する	ホジする	to maintain, preserve
保磁力	ホジリョク	magnetic coercive force
保存	ホゾン	conservation
保存則	ホゾンソク	conservation law
保存の法則	ホゾンのホウソク	conservation law

SUPPLEMENTARY VOCABULARY USING A DEDICATED KANJI PAIR

The KANJI that form this pair will rarely be seen separately in solid-state physics material. They are more easily remembered as a pair.

捕獲	ホカク	trapping
自己捕獲	ジコホカク	self-trapping
自己捕獲現象	ジコホカクゲンショウ	self-trapping phenomenon

SUPPLEMENTARY VOCABULARY USING KANJI FROM CHAPTER 16

BCS基準状態	BCSキジュンジョウタイ	BCS ground state
規格化条件	キカクカジョウケン	normalization condition

EXERCISES

Ex. 6.1 Matching Japanese and English terms

( ) 保持する   ( ) 軸方向応力   ( ) アンダーソン局在
( ) 長軸   ( ) 横緩和時間   ( ) 横光学フォノン
( ) 主軸   ( ) 横光学モード   ( ) スピン・格子緩和時間
( ) 保存則   ( ) 電子数保存   ( ) 成長温度依存性
( ) 同軸   ( ) 局所電場   ( ) モード間緩和
( ) 感光度   ( ) 局在状態   ( ) 双極子分極率
( ) 保磁力   ( ) 温度依存性   ( ) 相対感受率
( ) 双曲線関数   ( ) 縦緩和時間   ( ) 飽和磁化の温度依存性
( ) 局在長   ( ) 電子親和力   ( ) 規格化条件
( ) 自己捕獲   ( ) 磁気双極子

1. principal axis
2. axial stress
3. photosensitivity
4. magnetic dipole
5. relative permittivity
6. hyperbolic function
7. coaxial
8. major axis
9. self-trapping
10. normalization condition
11. electron affinity
12. transverse optical mode
13. inter-mode relaxation
14. dipolar polarizability
15. temperature dependence
16. localized state
17. localization length
18. local (electric) field
19. magnetic coercive force
20. longitudinal relaxation time
21. conservation of electron number
22. growth temperature dependence
23. transverse relaxation time
24. transverse optical phonon
25. spin-lattice relaxation time
26. Anderson localization
27. temperature dependence of saturation magnetization
28. conservation law
29. to maintain, preserve

Ex. 6.2 Choosing the correct KANJI

1. (1)係   (2)依   ( )存   関( )
2. (1)構   (2)横   ( )造   ( )軸
3. (1)感   (2)成   ( )度   生( )
4. (1)縁   (2)緩   ( )和   絶( )
5. (1)局   (2)属   金( )   ( )在
6. (1)軌   (2)軸   ( )道   横( )
7. (1)縦   (2)織   組( )   ( )軸
8. (1)観   (2)親   ( )察   ( )和
9. (1)捕   (2)構   機( )   ( )獲

Ex. 6.3　Sentence translations

1. 分数量子ホール効果は垂直な磁場内の2次元荷電粒子系に付随した特有な物理の現れである。
2. 二次元電子系の強磁場中の対角伝導率の測定は、1966年IBMグループによって、コルビーノ円板形状をもつシリコンMOSFETを用いて行われた。
3. 安藤、松本と植村の1975年の論文はいくつかの近似で進められていった。その最初の結果は、ホール伝導率σ_{xy}は、サイクロトロン角振動数ω_c、ランダウ準位幅Γと対角伝導率σ_{xx}を用い$\sigma_{xy} = -Ne/B + (2\pi\Gamma/h\omega_c)\sigma_{xx}$と表された。
4. 酸化物超伝導体の性質はそれに含まれるホール・キャリアの濃度に大きく依存する。

付随する	フズイする	to accompany	植村	うえむら	Uemura {surname}
特有な	トクユウな	characteristic	論文	ロンブン	scientific paper
年	ネン	year	近似	キンジ	approximation
円板	エンバン	disk	対角	タイカク	diagonal
安藤	アンドウ	Ando {surname}	超伝導体	チョウデンドウタイ	superconductor
松本	まつもと	Matsumoto {surname}			

Ex. 6.4　Paragraph translations—metals and insulators

1.　金属の自由電子モデルは金属の比熱、熱伝導率、電気伝導率、磁化率、電気力学に対してかなりの理解を与えた。しかし、このモデルは次のような他の多くの疑問に対しては答えられなかった。金属と半金属と半導体と絶縁体との区別；ホール定数が正の値をとる場合が生ずること；金属の伝導電子と自由原子の価電子との関係；多くの輸送現象の性質、特に磁場内での輸送現象。自由電子モデルほど素朴でない理論が必要であると思われる。幸いなことに、自由電子モデルを改良しようとするどんな簡単な試みも、ほとんどの場合、非常によい結果を生むことがわかったのである。

2.　よい導体とよい絶縁体との差は驚くべきほど大きい。純粋な金属の電気抵抗の値は1Kにおいては、超伝導体となる可能性を除いて、$10^{-10}\Omega$cmほどにまで低い。よい絶縁体の抵抗は$10^{22}\Omega$cmほども高い。固体のどの普通の物理的性質を考えてみても、10^{32}という範囲は最も幅が広いと思われる。

3.　絶縁体と導体との区別を理解するためには、自由電子モデルを固体の周期格子を考慮して拡張しなければならない。そのために生ずる最も重要な新しい性質はエネルギーギャップの出現する可能性である。結晶内の電子が示す他の非常に著しい性質は次のものである。結晶内電子に電場または磁場を加えると、それらは場に対してあたかも有効質量をもつ電子であるかのように応答する。有効質量は自由電子の質量よりも大きいこともあるし、小さいこともあるばかりでなく、負になることさえある。結晶内の電子は加えられた場に対して、負あるいは正の電荷をもつかのように応答する。ホール定数が負の値や正の値をもったりすることはこのことで説明される。

4. もし価電子が一つか、あるいはいくつかのバンドを完全に満たし、他のバンドを空にしているならば、結晶は絶縁体となる。外から加えた電場は絶縁体の中に電流を生じさせない。(電場は電子構造を乱すほどには強くないと仮定する。)電子によって満たされたバンドが、次に高いバンドからエネルギーギャップによって隔てられているならば、電子は異なる電子状態に移ることができないので、電子の全運動量を連続的に変化させる方法はないのである。電場が加えられても、何の変化も生じない。これは自由電子に対しては全く起こりえない状態である。自由電子のkは電場の中で一様に増加する。

5. 伝導率のもっとも簡単な理論は半古典的で、量子力学は極めて間接的に入ってくる。それは平均自由時間τ_0および(または)平均自由行程l_0の概念に基づく。この考え方では、電荷 $-e$、フェルミ速度v_Fをもつ電子は散乱されてその平均値がゼロであるような新しい速度になるまでに平均距離 $l_0 = v_F \tau_0$ だけ進む。もし電子(質量m)が弱い電場Eの中にあるならば、その速度は衝突と衝突との間に平均的 $\Delta v = -eE\tau_0/m$ だけ増加するであろう。すべての電子からの寄与を加え合わせて、電流密度 $j = \sigma_0 E$ となる。ここでσ_0は有名な式

$$\sigma_0 = ne^2\tau_0/m^*$$

で与えられ、nは電子数密度である。量子結果は、電子の質量m_eをその有効質量m^*に変えるところのバンド構造、およびτ_0の値を通して入ってくる。また、パウリの原理はフェルミ面近傍の電子だけが活動的であることを要求する。しかし独立電子近似においては、この効果は上の式を変えない。

疑問	ギモン	doubt		完全に	カンゼンに	perfectly
価電子	カデンシ	valence electron		乱す	みだす	to disturb
素朴	ソボク	simple		仮定する	カテイする	to assume, suppose
理論	リロン	theory		隔てる	へだてる	to separate, interpose
幸いな	さいわいな	fortunate				
改良する	カイリョウする	to improve		何の...も ...ない	なんの...も ...ない	there is no ... at all
驚くべき	おどろくべき	astonishingly				
範囲	ハンイ	range		弱い	よわい	weak
低い	ひくい	low		寄与	キヨ	contribution
考慮する	コウリョする	to think, consider		有名な	ユウメイな	famous
拡張する	カクチョウする	to expand, extend		近傍	キンボウ	neighborhood, vicinity
出現する	シュツゲンする	to emerge, appear				
著しい	いちじるしい	remarkable		活動的	カツドウテキ	active
あたかも		just like, just as		独立	ドクリツ	independent

Translations for Ex. 6.3

1. The fractional quantum Hall effect is an expression of the characteristic physics of two-dimensional systems of charged particles in a perpendicular magnetic field.
2. Measurements of the diagonal conductivity of a two-dimensional electron system in a strong magnetic field were performed in 1966 by an IBM group using a silicon MOSFET in the form of a Corbino disk.
3. A 1975 paper by Ando, Matsumoto, and Uemura was able to make progress using several approximations. Their first result showed that the Hall conductivity σ_{xy} can be expressed in terms of the cyclotron angular frequency ω_c, the width of the Landau level Γ, and the diagonal conductivity σ_{xx} as $\sigma_{xy} = -Ne/B + (2\pi\Gamma/h\omega_c)\sigma_{xx}$.
4. The properties of oxide superconductors strongly depend on the density of Hall carriers that they contain.

Translations for Ex. 6.4

1. The free electron model for metals gives a good understanding with respect to metallic specific heat, thermal conductivity, electrical conductivity, magnetic susceptibility, and electrodynamics. However, this model was unable to respond to other questions such as: the distinction between metals, semi-metals, semiconductors, and insulators; the occasional appearance of a positive Hall constant ; the relationship between the conduction electrons of metals and the valence electrons of free atoms; many transport properties; and especially transport phenomena in a magnetic field. A theory is required, one that is not as simple as the free-electron model. Fortunately, it has turned out that in most cases even simple attempts to improve the free-electron model have produced extremely good results.

2. The difference between good conductors and good insulators is astonishingly large. If we exclude the possibility of becoming superconductors, the value of electrical resistance of pure metals at temperatures of 1K is as low as $10^{-10}\Omega$-cm. The resistance of good insulators is as high as 10^{22} Ω-cm. This wide range of 10^{32} is considered to be the widest span among the ordinary physical properties of solids.

3. In order to understand the distinction between an insulator and a conductor, we must expand the free electron model and consider the periodic lattice of the solid. The most important new characteristic produced is the possibility of the emergence of an energy gap. Another extremely remarkable property which is displayed by electrons within a crystal is the following. When electric or magnetic fields are applied to electrons within a crystal, the response to the field is just as though the electrons have an effective mass. Not only can the effective mass be larger or smaller than the free-electron mass, but it can even be negative. The response of the electrons within the crystal to the applied field is as if they have negative or positive charge. This can explain why the Hall constant can have negative and positive values.

4. A crystal becomes an insulator if valence electrons completely fill one or several bands, and other bands are empty. An externally applied electric field is unable to produce a current within an insulator (assuming that the electric field is not so strong as to disturb the electron structure). If a band which is filled with electrons is separated from the next higher band by an energy gap, the electrons are unable to move to a different electron state. Thus, there is no way for the total momentum of the electrons to continuously change. Even if an electric field is applied, no change whatsoever is produced. This is a state that cannot occur at all for free electrons. The free electron **k** smoothly increases under the action of an electric field.

5. The simplest theory of conductivity is semi-classical, and quantum mechanics enters into it very indirectly. It is conceptually based on a mean-free time τ_0 and/or a mean-free path l_0. In this approach, an electron with an electric charge $-e$ and a Fermi velocity v_F is scattered to a new mean velocity near zero, and advances only a mean distance $l_0 = v_F \tau_0$. If the electron (of mass m) is in a weak electric field E, on the average the velocity of the electron will probably increase between collisions by only $\Delta v = -eE\tau_0/m$. Adding together the contributions from all electrons, the electric current density becomes $j = \sigma_0 E$. Here, σ_0 is given by the well-known equation

$$\sigma_0 = ne^2\tau_0/m^*$$

where n is the electron number density. Quantum effects enter via the band structure changing the electron mass m into its effective mass m^*, and via the value of τ_0. Also, the Pauli principle demands that only the electrons in the vicinity of the Fermi surface are active. However, in the independent electron approximation this effect does not change the above equation.

維	イ	rope
拡	カク	spreading, expanding
群	グン	group
称	ショウ	symmetry
繊	セン	fine, slender
操	ソウ	steering, operating
束	ソク	bundle; flux
凍	トウ	freezing
縛	バク / しば(る)	binding, constraint / to bind, tie up
模	ボ；モ	model, pattern

維 拡
群 称
繊 操
束 凍
縛 模

53

維

維持する	イジする	to maintain
繊維光学	センイコウガク	fiber optics

拡

拡散	カクサン	diffusion
拡散係数	カクサンケイスウ	diffusion coefficient
拡散度	カクサンド	diffusivity
拡散律速	カクサンリッソク	diffusion rate
拡大	カクダイ	enlargement
拡大率	カクダイリツ	magnifying power
拡張ゾーン形式	カクチョウゾーンケイシキ	expanded zone scheme
自己拡散	ジコカクサン	self-diffusion

群

群速度	グンソクド	group velocity
群論	グンロン	group theory
結晶点群	ケッショウテングン	crystal point group
点群操作	テングンソウサ	point group operation
点群対称性	テングンタイショウセイ	point group symmetry

称

鏡映対称	キョウエイタイショウ	reflection symmetry
対称	タイショウ	(geometric) symmetry
対称軸	タイショウジク	axis of symmetry
点群対称性	テングンタイショウセイ	point group symmetry

繊

合成繊維	ゴウセイセンイ	synthetic fiber
繊維光学	センイコウガク	fiber optics

操

回転操作	カイテンソウサ	rotation operation
格子並進操作	コウシヘイシンソウサ	lattice translation operation
鏡映操作	キョウエイソウサ	reflection operation
顕微操作	ケンビソウサ	micromanipulation
単位操作	タンイソウサ	unit operation
点群操作	テングンソウサ	point group operation
反転操作	ハンテンソウサ	inversion operation
並進操作	ヘイシンソウサ	translation operation

束

強束縛の近似	キョウソクバクのキンジ	tight-binding approximation
磁束の量子化	ジソクのリョウシカ	quantization of magnetic flux
磁束量子	ジソクリョウシ	flux quantum
束縛エネルギー	ソクバクエネルギー	binding energy
不純物の束縛エネルギー	フジュンブツのソクバクエネルギー	impurity binding energy
励起子の束縛エネルギー	レイキシのソクバクエネルギー	exciton binding energy

凍

軌道角運動量の凍結	キドウカクウンドウリョウのトウケツ	quenching of orbital angular momentum
凍結	トウケツ	quenching

縛

強束縛の近似	キョウソクバクのキンジ	tight-binding approximation
束縛エネルギー	ソクバクエネルギー	binding energy
不純物の束縛エネルギー	フジュンブツのソクバクエネルギー	impurity binding energy
励起子の束縛エネルギー	レイキシのソクバクエネルギー	exciton binding energy

模

規模	キボ	scale (in size)
クローニッヒ・ペニー模型	クローニッヒ・ペニーモケイ	Kronig-Penny model
模型	モケイ	(scale) model
模式的に	モシキテキに	schematically
模造の	モゾウの	imitation, artificial
模様	モヨウ	pattern

SUPPLEMENTARY VOCABULARY USING DEDICATED KANJI PAIRS

The KANJI that form these pairs will rarely be seen separately in solid-state physics material. They are more easily remembered as pairs.

干渉	カンショウ	interference
干渉効果	カンショウコウカ	interference effect
量子力学的	リョウシリキガクテキ	quantum mechanical
干渉効果	カンショウコウカ	interference effect
古典	コテン	classic(al)
金属の古典電子論	キンゾクのコテンデンシロン	classical electron theory of metals
古典電子論	コテンデンシロン	classical electron theory
電子分極率の	デンシブンキョクリツの	classical theory of electronic
古典論	コテンロン	polarizability
摩擦	マサツ	friction
摩擦の効果	マサツのコウカ	effect of friction

SUPPLEMENTARY VOCABULARY USING KANJI FROM CHAPTER 17

安定化	アンテイカ	stabilization
依然として	イゼンとして	still now, as before
一様分布	イチヨウブンプ	uniform distribution
井戸型ポテンシャル	いどがたポテンシャル	well-shaped potential
ウッド記号	ウッドキゴウ	Wood symbol
演算子	エンザンシ	operator
概算	ガイサン	rough estimate
回転軸	カイテンジク	axis of rotation
概論	ガイロン	general remarks, outline
換算質量	カンサンシツリョウ	reduced mass
規準座標変換	キジュンザヒョウヘンカン	standard coordinate transformation
ゲージ変換	ゲージヘンカン	gauge transformation
検査	ケンサ	inspection
交換エネルギー	コウカンエネルギー	exchange energy
自然科学	シゼンカガク	natural sciences
自然放出光スペクトル	シゼンホウシュツコウ スペクトル	natural emission spectrum
準結晶	ジュンケッショウ	quasicrystal
走査型電子顕微鏡	ソウサがたデンシケンビキョウ	scanning electron microscope (SEM)
双晶変形	ソウショウヘンケイ	twinning
ダブルヘテロ型 量子井戸	ダブルヘテロがた リョウシいど	double hetero(structure)-type of quantum well

適切な	テキセツな	appropriate, pertinent
転位	テンイ	dislocation
転位の上昇運動	テンイのジョウショウウンドウ	dislocation climbing
転位リング	テンイリング	dislocation ring
電子分布	デンシブンプ	electron distribution
動径分布関数	ドウケイブンプカンスウ	radial distribution function
パイエルス不安定	パイエルスフアンテイ	Peierls instability
刃状転位	はジョウテンイ	edge dislocation
刃状転位の運動	はジョウテンイのウンドウ	edge dislocation movement
刃状転位の弾性 エネルギー	はジョウテンイのダンセイ エネルギー	elastic energy of edge dislocation
光検出器	ひかりケンシュツキ	optical detector
光双安定スイッチ 現象	ひかりソウアンテイスイッチ ゲンショウ	optical bi-stable switching phenomenon
光双安定デバイス	ひかりソウアンテイデバイス	optical bi-stable device
フェルミ・ディラックの 分布関数	フェルミ・ディラックの ブンプカンスウ	Fermi-Dirac distribution function
分散曲線	ブンサンキョクセン	dispersion curve
ポテンシャル分布	ポテンシャルブンプ	potential distribution
ボルツマン分布	ボルツマンブンプ	Boltzmann distribution
マクスウェル分布	マクスウェルブンプ	Maxwell distribution
マグノンの分散関数	マグノンのブンサンカンスウ	magnon dispersion function
ミスフィット転位	ミスフィットテンイ	misfit dislocation
ヤーン・テラー効果	ヤーン・テラーコウカ	Jahn-Teller effect

EXERCISES

Ex. 7.1 Matching Japanese and English terms—group theory vocabulary

( ) 群論　　　　　　( ) 点群対称性　　　( ) 対称
( ) 回転操作　　　　( ) 並進操作　　　　( ) 規準座標変換
( ) 結晶点群　　　　( ) 反転操作　　　　( ) ゲージ変換
( ) 単位操作　　　　( ) 点群操作　　　　( ) 鏡映操作
( ) 対称軸　　　　　( ) 回転軸　　　　　( ) 鏡映対称

1. axis of rotation
2. reflection symmetry
3. unit operation
4. inversion operation
5. group theory
6. reflection operation
7. (geometric) symmetry
8. point group symmetry
9. axis of symmetry
10. gauge transformation
11. point group operation
12. translation operation
13. rotation operation
14. crystal point group
15. standard coordinate transformation

Ex. 7.2 Matching Japanese and English terms—子 words

( ) 因子　　　　　　( ) 磁子　　　　　　( ) 分子
( ) 演算子　　　　　( ) 準粒子　　　　　( ) 粒子
( ) 原子　　　　　　( ) 双極子　　　　　( ) 量子
( ) 格子　　　　　　( ) 振り子　　　　　( ) 励起子
( ) 電子

1. atom
2. (Bohr) magneton
3. dipole
4. electron
5. quantum
6. exciton
7. factor
8. lattice
9. molecule
10. operator
11. particle
12. pendulum
13. quasiparticle

Ex. 7.3 Matching Japanese and English terms—mixed KANA and KANJI terms

(　) 拡張ゾーン形式
(　) 転位リング
(　) 束縛エネルギー
(　) 交換エネルギー
(　) ウッド記号
(　) パイエルス不安定
(　) ミスフィット転位
(　) ボルツマン分布
(　) 光検出器
(　) ポテンシャル分布

(　) クローニッヒ・ペニー模型
(　) マグノンの分散関数
(　) フェルミ・ディラックの分布関数
(　) 不純物の束縛エネルギー
(　) 刃状転位の弾性エネルギー
(　) 励起子の束縛エネルギー
(　) ヤーン・テラー効果
(　) ダブルヘテロ型量子井戸
(　) マクスウェル分布
(　) 自然放出光スペクトル

1. Jahn-Teller effect
2. exchange energy
3. dislocation ring
4. binding energy
5. misfit dislocation
6. expanded zone scheme
7. Kronig-Penny model
8. Maxwell distribution
9. optical detector
10. Wood symbol

11. elastic energy of edge dislocation
12. Fermi-Dirac distribution function
13. impurity binding energy
14. magnon dispersion function
15. Boltzmann distribution
16. exciton binding energy
17. Peierls instability
18. potential distribution
19. natural emission spectrum
20. double hetero(structure)-type of quantum well

Ex. 7.4 Matching Japanese and English terms—other words

( ) 繊維光学　　　　( ) 維持する　　　　( ) 磁束の量子化
( ) 干渉　　　　　　( ) 拡散度　　　　　( ) 磁束量子
( ) 規模　　　　　　( ) 模造の　　　　　( ) 軌道角運動量の凍結
( ) 凍結　　　　　　( ) 拡大率　　　　　( ) 拡散係数
( ) 拡散　　　　　　( ) 自己拡散　　　　( ) 量子力学的干渉効果
( ) 拡大　　　　　　( ) 群速度　　　　　( ) 干渉効果
( ) 合成繊維　　　　( ) 顕微操作　　　　( ) 強束縛の近似
( ) 模型　　　　　　( ) 拡散律速　　　　( ) 電子分極率の古典論
( ) 摩擦　　　　　　( ) 準結晶　　　　　( ) 古典電子論
( ) 模様　　　　　　( ) 刃状転位　　　　( ) 金属の古典電子論
( ) 古典　　　　　　( ) 分散曲線　　　　( ) 光双安定スイッチ現象
( ) 安定化　　　　　( ) 依然として　　　( ) 走査型電子顕微鏡
( ) 転位　　　　　　( ) 電子分布　　　　( ) 転位の上昇運動
( ) 双晶変形　　　　( ) 動径分布関数　　( ) 光双安定デバイス
( ) 概算　　　　　　( ) 一様分布　　　　( ) 井戸型ポテンシャル
( ) 検査　　　　　　( ) 適切な　　　　　( ) 換算質量
( ) 概論　　　　　　( ) 自然科学　　　　( ) 刃状転位の運動

1. pattern	18. flux quantum	35. quantum mechanical interference effect
2. diffusivity	19. fiber optics	36. tight-binding approximation
3. to maintain	20. self-diffusion	37. classical theory of electronic polarizability
4. enlargement	21. diffusion rate	38. quantization of magnetic flux
5. scale (in size)	22. diffusion coefficient	39. optical bi-stable switching phenomenon
6. quenching	23. interference effect	40. classical electron theory
7. magnifying power	24. group velocity	41. (scale) model
8. synthetic fiber	25. micromanipulation	42. imitation, artificial
9. diffusion	26. friction	43. quenching of orbital angular momentum
10. interference	27. quasicrystal	44. classical electron theory of metals
11. twinning	28. appropriate, pertinent	45. optical bi-stable device
12. dislocation	29. uniform distribution	46. radial distribution function
13. classical	30. rough estimate	47. scanning electron microscope (SEM)
14. dispersion curve	31. dislocation climbing	48. well-shaped potential
15. reduced mass	32. natural sciences	49. still now, as before
16. inspection	33. electron distribution	50. edge dislocation movement
17. stabilization	34. edge dislocation	51. general remarks, outline, introduction

Ex. 7.5 Sentence translations

1. クーパー対の形成は、二つのフェルミ粒子でできたボーズ粒子が重心の運動量がゼロとなる状態にボーズ凝縮した状態と考えることができる。

2. 通常の電気的な物性は、固体中にある元素を質量の異なる同位元素で置換しても影響されない。

3. もし、超伝導状態で温度に比例する比熱が、試料中に残っているかもしれない常伝導不純物相などによるものではなく、真に超伝導をひき起こしている電子系固有の比熱であれば、このオルソI相ではBCS理論の枠を越えたまったく新しい機構による超伝導が実現していることになる。

4. 1電子モデルによると、基本単位格子あたり1個の水素原子からなる結晶では、常に半分だけ占有されたエネルギーバンドが存在し、そのなかでの電荷の輸送が可能である。

5. 超伝導体の内部ではB＝0となるといったが、これは巨視的に見たときの話で、微視的に見ると図に模式的に示したように超伝導体の表面近傍ではBの大きさが空間変化し、距離λ程度超伝導体の内部に入るとBがほとんど零になる。このλを侵入深さと呼ぶ。

凝縮する	ギョウシュクする	to condense, coagulate	占有する	センユウする	to occupy
試料	シリョウ	sample, test material	巨視的に	キョシテキに	macroscopically
			話	はなし	story, tale
真に	シンに	actually, in fact	微視的に	ビシテキに	microscopically
枠	わく	framework	侵入	シンニュウ	penetration
越える	こえる	to transcend	深さ	ふかさ	depth
			呼ぶ	よぶ	to name, call

Ex. 7.6 Paragraph translations

1. スイス・チューリッヒのIBM研究所のベドノルツ博士とミュラー博士の画期的な発見により、高温超伝導体開発が世界的な規模で展開されることとなった。この発見の意義は、1974年以来23Kに留まっていたT_cの記録値を一気に30Kまで引き上げたというだけではない。それ以上に重要なことは、従来の金属間化合物超伝導体とは多くの点で異なった性質をもつ酸化物超伝導体で、金属間化合物を凌ぐ高温超伝導を見出したことであろう。超伝導体開発の歴史を振り返ってみると、T_cの記録値対年度を示す図からも明らかなように、その対象となる物質は、元素、合金、二元系金属間化合物、さらに三元系金属間化合物へと展開されてきた。ここで酸化物超伝導体が華々しく登場し、新しい酸化物時代が始まろうとしているのである。

2. 超伝導という現象が初めて人類の前にその姿を現したのは、抵抗が零になる現象を通じてである。この現象は1911年、オランダのカマリング・オンネスによって見出された。1913年のノーベル賞受賞講演で発表された実験データが図に示してある。水銀の電気抵抗が4K程度の温度以下で消失していることが見える。当時は、量子力学誕生以前であり、温度が下がって絶対零度に近づいたときに抵抗の値がどうなるかについて

61

はいろいろの考えがあった。カマリング・オンネスは、彼が開発したヘリウムの液化機を用いてつくった液体ヘリウムにいろいろな金属を浸しているうちにこの発見をした。この抵抗が消失する温度、すなわち、超伝導が出現する温度は臨界温度と呼ばれ、通常、T_c と書かれる。

博士	ハクシ	Ph.D.	華々しい	はなばなしい	glorious, brilliant
画期的な	カッキテキな	epoch-making	登場する	トウジョウする	to appear (on stage)
世界的な	セカイテキな	global	始まる	はじまる	to begin {v.i.}
展開する	テンカイする	to develop, unfold	初めて	はじめて	for the first time
意義	イギ	significance, importance	姿	すがた	form
			賞	ショウ	prize
以来	イライ	(ever) since	講演	コウエン	lecture
留まる	とどまる	to stop, halt {v.i.}	誕生	タンジョウ	birth
記録値	キロクチ	record (value)	近づく	ちかづく	to approach {v.i.}
一気に	イッキに	all at once	彼	かれ	he
凌ぐ	しのぐ	to withstand, surpass	浸す	ひたす	to immerse, soak
			臨界	リンカイ	critical (temperature)
歴史	レキシ	history			
振り返える	ふりかえる	to turn around, look back	書く	かく	to write

(*Note*: 博士 is read ハカセ in some situations.)

(*Note*: 浸 used in Ex. 7.6 must be distinguished from 侵 given in Ex. 7.5.)

Translations for Ex. 7.5

1. The formation of Cooper pairs can be thought of in terms of a Bose condensed state of Bose particles made from pairs of Fermi particles in states of zero center-of-mass momentum.
2. Ordinary electrical properties are not influenced when isotopes of differing mass are substituted for an element in a solid.
3. If the specific heat in the superconducting state is proportional to temperature and it is not due to causes such as the normally conducting impurity phases in the sample material, and if it is actually the characteristic specific heat of the electron system giving rise to superconductivity, then it may turn out that in this ortho-I phase an entirely new mechanism for superconductivity has been realized that goes beyond the framework of the BCS theory.
4. In the single-electron model, for a crystal made up of one hydrogen atom per primitive unit cell, energy bands will exist that are only half-filled, and there is the possibility of transport of electric charge within them.
5. We have stated that within a superconductor B equals zero, but this is the story when viewed macroscopically. As shown schematically in the figure, when viewed microscopically the magnitude of B varies spatially in the vicinity of the surface of the superconductor, and becomes nearly zero within a distance λ into the interior of the superconductor. This λ is called the penetration depth.

Translations for Ex. 7.6

1. After the epoch-making discovery in Zürich, Switzerland, by IBM research laboratory scientists Drs. Bednorz and Müller, the development of high-temperature superconductors came about on a global scale. The significance of this discovery is not just that it abruptly raised the record value for T_c from 23 K, where it had been stalled since 1974, to 30 K. Probably more important than that, was the discovery of oxide superconductors, which have properties that differ in numerous ways from conventional intermetallic superconductors and can surpass them. When we reflect upon the history of the discovery of superconductors as elucidated by the figure showing the record T_c year by year, this unfolded as the materials under study progressed from element, to alloy, to binary intermetallic compounds, and then to tertiary intermetallic compounds. At this point, oxide superconductors gloriously take center stage, and a new oxide era is about to begin.

2. The form of the phenomenon called superconductivity first appeared to mankind through the zero resistance phenomenon. It was discovered in 1911 by Kamerlingh Onnes of the Netherlands, and the experimental data presented in his 1913 Nobel Prize acceptance lecture is shown in the figure. The disappearance of the electrical resistance of mercury at about 4 K and lower is visible. That happened before the birth of quantum mechanics, and there were various ideas regarding what would become of the value of electrical resistance as temperatures were lowered close to absolute zero. Kamerlingh Onnes made discoveries by immersing various metals in liquid helium made using a helium liquifier he had developed. The temperature where resistance disappears, namely where superconductivity appears, is called the critical temperature, and is ordinarily written as T_c.

殻	カク	shell
	から	shell

源	ゲン	source; origin

止	シ	stopping
	と (める)	to stop {v.t.}
	と (まる)	to stop {v.i.}

紫	シ	violet
	むらさき	purple, violet

乗	ジョウ	power, multiplication
	ジョウ (じる)	to multiply {math}

整	セイ	arranging in order
	ととの (える)	to put in order {v.t.}
	ととの (う)	to be arranged {v.i.}

短	タン	short
	みじか (い)	short

偏	ヘン	one-sided, biased
	ヘン-	partial {math}
	ヘン-	polarized

網	モウ	net, network
	あみ	net, network

絡	ラク	connection

殻　源
止　紫
乗　整
短　偏
網　絡

殻

空殻モデル	クウカクモデル	empty shell model
閉殻構造	ヘイカクコウゾウ	closed shell structure

源

音源	オンゲン	sound source
起源	キゲン	origin, beginning
光源	コウゲン	light source
資源	シゲン	resource
電源	デンゲン	electrical power source
熱源	ネツゲン	heat source
フランク・リードの 転位源	フランク・リードの テンイゲン	Frank-Reed dislocation source

止

禁止帯	キンシタイ	forbidden band
静止ドメイン	セイシドメイン	stationary domain
中止する	チュウシする	to stop, shut down

紫

紫外光	シガイコウ	ultraviolet light
紫外光電子分光	シガイコウデンシブンコウ	ultraviolet photoelectron spectroscopy (UPS)

乗

三乗	サンジョウ	cubed, third power
乗法群	ジョウホウグン	multiplicative group
二乗	ニジョウ	squared, second power

整

整数	セイスウ	integer
整理	セイリ	arrangement
整流器	セイリュウキ	rectifier
整流特性	セイリュウトクセイ	rectification
積層不整	セキソウフセイ	random stacking
調整	チョウセイ	adjustment

短

高周波短絡 条件	コウシュウハタンラク ジョウケン	high-frequency, short-circuit conditions
短距離規則度	タンキョリキソクド	short-range order
短距離規則度 パラメーター	タンキョリキソクド パラメーター	short-range order parameter
短軸	タンジク	minor axis
短時定数	タンジテイスウ	short time constant
短絡	タンラク	short circuit

偏

偏向	ヘンコウ	deflection
偏光	ヘンコウ	polarized light
偏波面依存性	ヘンパメンイゾンセイ	polarization plane dependence
偏波面の選択性	ヘンパメンのセンタクセイ	polarization plane selectivity
偏微分	ヘンビブン	partial differential

網

網構造	あみコウゾウ	net structure
基準網構造	キジュンあみコウゾウ	base net structure
斜交網構造	シャコウあみコウゾウ	oblique net structure
単位網目	タンイあみめ	mesh
ランダム網目構造	ランダムあみめコウゾウ	random network

絡

高周波短絡 条件	コウシュウハタンラク ジョウケン	high-frequency, short-circuit conditions
短絡	タンラク	short circuit
包絡関数	ホウラクカンスウ	envelope function
包絡線	ホウラクセン	envelope (of a waveform)

SUPPLEMENTARY VOCABULARY USING DEDICATED KANJI PAIRS

The KANJI that form these pairs will rarely be seen separately in solid-state physics material. They are more easily remembered as pairs.

敷居	しきい	threshold
敷居値電圧	しきいチデンアツ	threshold voltage
敷居値電流密度	しきいチデンリュウミツド	threshold current density
遮蔽	シャヘイ	screening
遮蔽距離	シャヘイキョリ	screening distance
遮蔽されたクーロン・ポテンシャル	シャヘイされたクーロン・ポテンシャル	screened Coulomb potential
静電的遮蔽	セイデンテキシャヘイ	electrostatic screening
トーマス・フェルミの遮蔽距離	トーマス・フェルミのシャヘイキョリ	Thomas-Fermi screening length (distance)

SUPPLEMENTARY VOCABULARY USING KANJI FROM CHAPTER 18

アルベーン波	アルベーンハ	Alfvén wave
回折強度	カイセツキョウド	diffraction strength
回折ビーム	カイセツビーム	diffracted beam
凝縮	ギョウシュク	condensation
禁制帯幅	キンセイタイはば	forbidden band width
空間電荷波	クウカンデンカハ	space charge wave
空間電荷波の振る舞い	クウカンデンカハのふるまい	behavior of the space charge wave
クーロン散乱	クーロンサンラン	Coulomb scattering
屈折率スペクトル	クッセツリツスペクトル	refractivity spectrum
後方散乱スペクトル	コウホウサンランスペクトル	backscattering spectrum
雑音	ザツオン	noise, static
サブバンド間散乱	サブバンドカンサンラン	inter-sub-band scattering
散乱機構	サンランキコウ	scattering mechanism
散乱ベクトル	サンランベクトル	scattering vector
持続波変調	ジゾクハヘンチョウ	continuous wave modulation
状態図	ジョウタイズ	state diagram
振動電流波形	シンドウデンリュウハケイ	current oscillation waveform
正常散乱	セイジョウサンラン	regular scattering
静電ポテンシャル	セイデンポテンシャル	electrostatic potential
単原子層	タンゲンシソウ	monatomic layer
弾性散乱	ダンセイサンラン	elastic scattering
弾性波の量子化	ダンセイハのリョウシカ	quantization of elastic waves
デバイの切断波動ベクトル	デバイのセツダンハドウベクトル	Debye cutoff wave vector

電磁波の分散式	デンジハのブンサンシキ	electromagnetic wave dispersion formula
波動関数	ハドウカンスウ	wave function
波動関数工学	ハドウカンスウコウガク	wave function engineering
波動ベクトル	ハドウベクトル	wave vector
反射電子線回折装置	ハンシャデンシセンカイセキソウチ	reflection electron beam diffraction apparatus
被変調波	ヒヘンチョウハ	modulated wave
負微分移動度の静特性	フビブンイドウのセイトクセイ	negative differential mobility static characteristic
複雑な	フクザツな	complicated, intricate
複写する	フクシャする	to duplicate, copy
ポラリトン散乱	ポラリトンサンラン	polariton scattering
予熱炉	ヨネツロ	preheating furnace
ラザフォード後方散乱	ラザフォードコウホウサンラン	Rutherford backscattering
量子波動エレクトロニクス	リョウシハドウエレクトロニクス	quantum wave electronics

EXERCISES

Ex. 8.1 Matching Japanese and English terms—words with common suffixes

( )　音源　　　　　　　( )　閉殻構造　　　　　( )　偏波面の選択性
( )　光源　　　　　　　( )　包絡関数　　　　　( )　斜交網構造
( )　整数　　　　　　　( )　短時定数　　　　　( )　高周波短絡条件
( )　熱源　　　　　　　( )　基準網構造　　　　( )　短距離規則度
( )　起源　　　　　　　( )　偏波面依存性　　　( )　敷居値電流密度
( )　電源　　　　　　　( )　整流特性　　　　　( )　負微分移動度の静特性
( )　整流器　　　　　　( )　網構造　　　　　　( )　電磁波の分散式

1. light source
2. envelope function
3. rectifier
4. heat source
5. net structure
6. integer
7. electrical power source
8. closed shell structure
9. threshold current density
10. oblique net structure
11. short-range order
12. origin, beginning
13. sound source
14. rectification
15. polarization plane selectivity
16. electromagnetic wave dispersion formula
17. high-frequency, short-circuit conditions
18. polarization plane dependence
19. base net structure
20. negative differential mobility static characteristic
21. short time constant

Ex. 8.2 Matching Japanese and English terms—mixed KANA and KANJI terms

( )　空殻モデル　　　　　　　( )　フランク・リードの転位源
( )　散乱ベクトル　　　　　　( )　トーマス・フェルミの遮蔽距離
( )　クーロン散乱　　　　　　( )　デバイの切断波動ベクトル
( )　静止ドメイン　　　　　　( )　遮蔽されたクーロン・ポテンシャル
( )　屈折率スペクトル　　　　( )　静電ポテンシャル
( )　回折ビーム　　　　　　　( )　後方散乱スペクトル
( )　サブバンド間散乱　　　　( )　ラザフォード後方散乱
( )　ポラリトン散乱　　　　　( )　短距離規則度パラメーター
( )　ランダム網目構造　　　　( )　量子波動エレクトロニクス

1. refractivity spectrum
2. Coulomb scattering
3. stationary domain
4. scattering vector
5. diffracted beam
6. empty shell model
7. random network
8. polariton scattering
9. quantum wave electronics
10. Frank-Reed dislocation source
11. screened Coulomb potential
12. inter-sub-band scattering
13. electrostatic potential
14. backscattering spectrum
15. short-range order parameter
16. Thomas-Fermi screening length
17. Debye cutoff wave vector
18. Rutherford backscattering

Ex. 8.3 Matching Japanese and English terms—other words

( ) 三乗　　　　　　　( ) 中止する　　　　　　( ) 紫外光電子分光
( ) 整理　　　　　　　( ) 禁止帯　　　　　　　( ) 弾性波の量子化
( ) 紫外光　　　　　　( ) 積層不整　　　　　　( ) 反射電子線回折装置
( ) 雑音　　　　　　　( ) 遮蔽距離　　　　　　( ) 空間電荷波の振る舞い
( ) 偏光　　　　　　　( ) 散乱機構　　　　　　( ) 持続波変調
( ) 調整　　　　　　　( ) 単位網目　　　　　　( ) 振動電流波形
( ) 包絡線　　　　　　( ) 乗法群　　　　　　　( ) 静電的遮蔽
( ) 偏向　　　　　　　( ) 複雑な　　　　　　　( ) 正常散乱
( ) 短軸　　　　　　　( ) 偏微分　　　　　　　( ) 敷居値電圧
( ) 予熱炉　　　　　　( ) 単原子層　　　　　　( ) 被変調波
( ) 弾性散乱　　　　　( ) 禁制帯幅　　　　　　( ) 空間電荷波

1. forbidden band
2. arrangement
3. cubed (math)
4. minor axis
5. noise, static
6. adjustment
7. mesh
8. deflection
9. modulated wave
10. monatomic layer
11. space charge wave
12. scattering mechanism
13. ultraviolet light
14. multiplicative group
15. random stacking
16. polarized light
17. partial differential
18. screening distance
19. regular scattering
20. preheating furnace
21. elastic scattering
22. threshold voltage
23. ultraviolet photoelectron spectroscopy (UPS)
24. to stop, shut down
25. quantization of elastic waves
26. electrostatic screening
27. behavior of the space charge wave
28. current oscillation waveform
29. complicated, intricate
30. continuous wave modulation
31. reflection electron beam diffraction apparatus
32. forbidden band width
33. envelope (of a waveform)

Ex. 8.4 Choosing the correct KANJI

1.	(1)蔽　(2)蒸	(　)気	遮(　)
2.	(1)散　(2)敷	(　)乱	(　)居
3.	(1)絡　(2)格	規(　)	短(　)
4.	(1)乗　(2)業	三(　)	作(　)
5.	(1)整　(2)装	(　)置	(　)理
6.	(1)短　(2)知	(　)能	(　)絡
7.	(1)選　(2)遮	(　)択	(　)蔽
8.	(1)局　(2)居	敷(　)	(　)在
9.	(1)殻　(2)般	一(　)	空(　)
10.	(1)網　(2)銅	(　)目	(　)線
11.	(1)原　(2)源	熱(　)	(　)理
12.	(1)止　(2)上	中(　)	(　)部
13.	(1)装　(2)紫	(　)外	(　)置
14.	(1)依　(2)偏	(　)光	(　)存性

Ex. 8.5 Sentence translations

1. $\varepsilon(0,K) = 1 + k_s^2/K^2$ に対する近似はトーマス・フェルミの誘電関数とよばれ、k_sは遮蔽パラメーターとよばれ、また$1/k_s$はトーマス・フェルミ遮蔽距離とよばれる。

2. 遮蔽されたクーロン・ポテンシャルは遮蔽された全ポテンシャルのフーリエ逆変換である。

3. 特に量子井戸レーザーでは、発振開始に必要な電流密度(敷居値電流密度)が通常型のレーザーの1/2かそれ以下まで低くできることが実験的にも理論的にも明らかにされてきた点は、極めて意義が大きい。

4. この種のトランジスターの応答時間は、すでに走行時間限界値(チャネル長を走行速度で除したもので、1–10ピコ秒)に近づきつつある。したがって、今後は、回路を複雑化させた場合にも、このような高速性を発揮させるためのデバイス研究などが重要となろう。これらの研究が進めば、量子効果の研究に端を発して生まれたヘテロ構造トランジスター群が、高度情報処理に不可欠な超高速デバイスとして、その地位を確保することとなろう。

誘電	ユウデン	dielectric	複雑化する	フクザツカする	to complicate
逆変換	ギャクヘンカン	inverse transform	発揮する	ハッキする	to exhibit,
開始	カイシ	the beginning, start			demonstrate
限界	ゲンカイ	limit, margin	不可欠な	フカケツな	indispensable
除する	ジョする	to divide {math}	地位	チイ	rank, status
秒	ビョウ	second			

Ex. 8.6　Paragraph translations

1．電子気体の中に埋まった一つの正電荷の電場は1/rよりも速く、rの増加とともに減少する。なぜなら、電子気体がまわりに集まって、この正電荷を遮蔽するからである。この静的遮蔽効果は静的誘電関数の波動ベクトル依存性によって記述される。印加された静電場に対する電子の応答を考察しよう。電荷密度が $-n_0 e$ である一様な電子気体が正の電荷密度 $n_0 e$ の背景と重なり合っている状態から出発する。いま正電荷の背景が力学的変形をうけてx方向に正弦関数形の電荷密度の変化を生じたとする。これを電子気体に加えられた外部電場と見なそう。

2．超伝導量子干渉素子は非常に磁束感度の高い超伝導素子であり、生体磁場のような微小磁場計測はもちろんのこと、古地磁気や資源探査のような地球物理学的計測、磁束量子の絶対測定のような電気精密計測、モノポールや重力波検出等の広い分野で使われている。中でも生体磁場計測は脳内の情報機能の研究のような科学的興味からばかりでなく、医療への応用からも大きな期待が寄せられている。

埋まる	うまる	to be buried	脳	ノウ	brain
印加する	インカする	to impress, apply	科学	カガク	science
背景	ハイケイ	background	興味	キョウミ	interest
正弦	セイゲン	sine {trigonometry}	医療	イリョウ	medical treatment
古地磁気	コジジキ	paleomagnetism	期待	キタイ	expectation
探査	タンサ	investigation, probe	寄せる	よせる	to gather together, bring about
精密	セイミツ	precision			

Translations for Ex. 8.5

1. The approximation $\varepsilon(0,K) = 1 + k_s^2/K^2$ is called the Thomas-Fermi dielectric function; k_s is called the screening parameter, and $1/k_s$ is called the Thomas-Fermi screening length.
2. The screened Coulomb potential is the inverse Fourier transform of the screened total potential.
3. For quantum well lasers in particular, it has been made clear experimentally and theoretically that the required current density for the beginning of oscillation, the threshold value of current density, can be reduced to half or less of that for ordinary lasers. This point is of very great significance.
4. The response time of this kind of transistor is already approaching the transit time limiting value (channel length divided by transit velocity, 1–10 picoseconds). Thus from now on, even with more complicated circuits, it will probably be important to do research on devices that can exhibit this kind of high speed behavior. If these research efforts move forward, heterostructure transistor families at the frontier of quantum effect research will likely have the indispensable super-high speed for advanced information processing, and will have secured their place therein.

Translations for Ex. 8.6

1. The electric field of a single positive charge buried in an electron gas decreases more rapidly than 1/r with increasing r. This is because the electron gas gathers around it and this positive charge is screened. This static screening effect can be described by the wave vector dependence of the static dielectric constant. Let us consider the electron response to this applied static electric field. We start from a state where a uniform electron gas which has a electric charge density of $-n_0e$ is superimposed upon a positive background charge density n_0e. Now, we suppose that the positive background charge is mechanically deformed and a sinusoidal variation of the charge density in the x direction is produced. This we shall regard as an external electric field that has been added to the electron gas.

2. A superconducting quantum interference device is a superconducting device with an extremely high flux sensitivity. It is being used in widespread fields such as, naturally, measurement of the minute magnetic fields in biomagnetism, geophysical measurements like those in paleomagnetism and resource exploration, precise measurements like the absolute measurement of the magnetic flux quantum, and the detection of monopoles and gravity waves. Of those, the biomagnetism measurements are not just for scientific interest in matters such as research on the information functions in the brain, but are also brought about by great expectations of applications in medical treatment.

希	キ	rare, dilute
視	シ	seeing
釈	シャク	essence
順	ジュン ジュン-	order; sequence forward (bias)
土	ト；ド つち	earth, ground earth, ground
膨	ボウ	swelling, expanding
鳴	メイ な(く) な(る)	making a sound to chirp, cry to ring, resound
輸	ユ	transporting
融	ユウ	fusing, melting
臨	リン	bordering on

希　視
釈　順
土　膨
鳴　輸
融　臨

希

He³・He⁴希釈 冷却器	He³・He⁴キシャク レイキャクキ	He³-He⁴ dilution refrigerator
希ガス	キガス	rare gas, inert gas, noble gas
希ガス結晶	キガスケッショウ	rare-gas crystal
希釈冷却	キシャクレイキャク	dilution refrigeration
希土類イオン	キドルイイオン	rare-earth ion
希土類元素	キドルイゲンソ	rare-earth element
希土類鉄ガーネット	キドルイテツガーネット	rare-earth iron garnet
希望	キボウ	wish, hope, desire

視

暗視野像	アンシヤゾウ	dark field image
可視光線	カシコウセン	visible light ray
巨視的な電場	キョシテキなデンば	macroscopic electric field
巨視的に	キョシテキに	macroscopically
注視	チュウシ	close observation, scrutiny
微視的な	ビシテキな	microscopic
明視野像	メイシヤゾウ	bright field image

釈

He³・He⁴希釈 冷却器	He³・He⁴キシャク レイキャクキ	He³-He⁴ dilution refrigerator
希釈冷却	キシャクレイキャク	dilution refrigeration

順

高界ドメイン繰り返し 順方向走行モード	コウカイドメインくりかえし ジュンホウコウソウコウ モード	repeating forward traveling mode in the high-field domain
順バイアス電圧	ジュンバイアスデンアツ	forward bias voltage
順方向電流	ジュンホウコウデンリュウ	forward current

土

アルカリ土類金属	アルカリドルイキンゾク	alkaline earth metal
希土類イオン	キドルイイオン	rare-earth ion
希土類元素	キドルイゲンソ	rare-earth element
希土類鉄ガーネット	キドルイテツガーネット	rare-earth iron garnet

膨

熱膨張	ネツボウチョウ	thermal expansion

鳴

核磁気共鳴	カクジキキョウメイ	nuclear magnetic resonance (NMR)
核四重極共鳴	カクシジュウキョクキョウメイ	nuclear quadrupole resonance (NQR)
強磁性共鳴	キョウジセイキョウメイ	ferromagnetic resonance
共鳴	キョウメイ	resonance
共鳴エネルギー	キョウメイエネルギー	resonance energy
共鳴器	キョウメイキ	resonator
共鳴光散乱	キョウメイひかりサンラン	resonant optical scattering
交換相互作用共鳴	コウカンソウゴサヨウキョウメイ	exchange interaction resonance
サイクロトロン共鳴	サイクロトロンキョウメイ	cyclotron resonance
サイクロトロン共鳴周波数	サイクロトロンキョウメイシュウハスウ	cyclotron resonance frequency
スピン波共鳴	スピンハキョウメイ	spin-wave resonance
電子常磁性共鳴	デンシジョウジセイキョウメイ	electron paramagnetic resonance (EPR)
二重障壁共鳴トンネルダイオード	ニジュウショウヘキキョウメイトンネルダイオード	double-barrier resonance tunnel diode
反強磁性共鳴	ハンキョウジセイキョウメイ	antiferromagnetic resonance
ヘリコン波の共鳴	ヘリコンハのキョウメイ	helicon wave resonance

輸

表面輸送現象	ヒョウメンユソウゲンショウ	surface transport phenomenon
ボルツマンの輸送方程式	ボルツマンのユソウホウテイシキ	Boltzmann transport equation
輸送	ユソウ	transport
輸送方程式	ユソウホウテイシキ	transport equation

融

共融温度	キョウユウオンド	eutectic temperature
共融合金	キョウユウゴウキン	eutectic alloy
融解	ユウカイ	fusion, melting, dissolution
融解熱	ユウカイネツ	heat of fusion
融点	ユウテン	melting point
溶融紡糸	ヨウユウボウシ	melt spinning

臨

下部臨界磁場	カブリンカイジば	lower critical magnetic field
上部臨界磁場	ジョウブリンカイジば	upper critical magnetic field
熱力学的臨界磁場	ネツリキガクテキリンカイジば	thermodynamic critical magnetic field
臨界温度	リンカイオンド	critical temperature
臨界現象	リンカイゲンショウ	critical phenomena
臨界質量	リンカイシツリョウ	critical mass
臨界磁場	リンカイジば	critical magnetic field
臨界ずれ歪み	リンカイずれひずみ	critical shear strain
臨界流速	リンカイリュウソク	critical flow velocity

SUPPLEMENTARY VOCABULARY USING DEDICATED KANJI PAIRS

The KANJI that form these pairs will rarely be seen separately in solid-state physics material. They are more easily remembered as pairs.

繰り返し	くりかえし	repeating
高界ドメイン繰り返し順方向走行モード	コウカイドメインくりかえしジュンホウコウソウコウモード	repeating forward traveling mode in the high-field domain
高界ドメイン繰り返し逆方向走行モード	コウカイドメインくりかえしギャクホウコウソウコウモード	repeating backward traveling mode in the high-field domain
占拠	センキョ	occupation
占拠数逆転	センキョスウギャクテン	population inversion
秩序	チツジョ	order, sequence
短距離秩序パラメーター	タンキョリチツジョパラメーター	short-range order parameter
秩序無秩序転移	チツジョムチツジョテンイ	order-disorder transition

SUPPLEMENTARY VOCABULARY USING KANJI FROM CHAPTER 19

価電子バンドの上端	カデンシバンドのジョウタン	upper edge of the valence band
逆電圧	ギャクデンアツ	reverse voltage
逆バイアス電圧	ギャクバイスデンアツ	reverse bias voltage
チェレンコフの限界	チェレンコフのゲンカイ	Cherenkov threshold
超伝導体の比熱	チョウデンドウタイのヒネツ	specific heat of a superconductor
超微細構造相互作用	チョウビサイコウゾウソウゴサヨウ	hyperfine structure interaction
ヘテロ界面	ヘテロカイメン	hetero-interface

EXERCISES

Ex. 9.1 Matching Japanese and English terms—resonance terms

( ) 核磁気共鳴　　　　　　　　　　( ) サイクロトロン共鳴周波数
( ) スピン波共鳴　　　　　　　　　( ) 電子常磁性共鳴
( ) 共鳴器　　　　　　　　　　　　( ) 核四重極共鳴
( ) 反強磁性共鳴　　　　　　　　　( ) 共鳴エネルギー
( ) 強磁性共鳴　　　　　　　　　　( ) 交換相互作用共鳴
( ) 共鳴光散乱　　　　　　　　　　( ) ヘリコン波の共鳴
( ) 二重障壁共鳴トンネルダイオード

1. spin-wave resonance
2. antiferromagnetic resonance
3. ferromagnetic resonance
4. resonance energy
5. helicon wave resonance
6. resonator
7. resonant optical scattering

8. nuclear quadrupole resonance (NQR)
9. electron paramagnetic resonance (EPR)
10. nuclear magnetic resonance (NMR)
11. cyclotron resonance frequency
12. exchange interaction resonance
13. double-barrier resonance tunnel diode

Ex. 9.2 Matching Japanese and English terms—mixed KANA and KANJI terms

( ) ヘテロ界面　　　　　　　　　　( ) 価電子バンドの上端
( ) 逆バイアス電圧　　　　　　　　( ) 境界面プラズモン
( ) 順バイアス電圧　　　　　　　　( ) 高界ドメイン繰り返し順方向走行モード
( ) チェレンコフの限界　　　　　　( ) 短距離秩序パラメーター
( ) アルカリ土類金属　　　　　　　( ) 高界ドメイン繰り返し逆方向走行モード
( ) 希土類鉄ガーネット　　　　　　( ) ボルツマンの輸送方程式

1. boundary plasmon
2. upper edge of the valence band
3. Cherenkov threshold
4. hetero-interface
5. alkaline earth metal
6. repeating forward traveling mode in the high-field domain
7. repeating backward traveling mode in the high-field domain
8. short-range order parameter
9. Boltzmann transport equation
10. reverse bias voltage
11. forward bias voltage
12. rare-earth iron garnet

Ex. 9.3 Matching Japanese and English terms—other words

( ) 可換群
( ) 軽量材
( ) 注視
( ) 希望
( ) 熱膨張
( ) 融点
( ) 臨界温度
( ) 微視的な
( ) 臨界流速
( ) 融解熱
( ) 臨界質量

( ) 暗視野像
( ) 臨界現象
( ) 順方向電流
( ) 下部臨界磁場
( ) 臨界磁場
( ) 共融合金
( ) 占拠数逆転
( ) 共融温度
( ) 明視野像
( ) 融解
( ) 溶融紡糸

( ) 希ガス結晶
( ) 希釈冷却
( ) 巨視的な電場
( ) 熱力学的臨界磁場
( ) 表面輸送現象
( ) 秩序無秩序転移
( ) 超伝導体の比熱
( ) 臨界ずれ歪み
( ) 可視光線
( ) 希土類元素

1. rare gas crystal
2. dark field image
3. commutative group
4. wish, hope, desire
5. melting point
6. eutectic alloy
7. critical mass
8. eutectic temperature
9. microscopic
10. melt spinning
11. bright field image
12. macroscopic electric field
13. dilution refrigeration
14. forward current
15. rare earth element
16. thermal expansion
17. critical temperature
18. population inversion
19. critical flow velocity
20. visible light ray
21. heat of fusion
22. critical shear strain
23. critical phenomenon
24. lightweight material
25. lower critical magnetic field
26. thermodynamic critical magnetic field
27. critical magnetic field
28. surface transport phenomenon
29. specific heat of a superconductor
30. order-disorder transition
31. close observation, scrutiny
32. fusion, melting, dissolution

Ex. 9.4 Choosing the correct KANJI

1. (1)輸 (2)論
2. (1)点 (2)占
3. (1)秩 (2)鉄
4. (1)螺 (2)融
5. (1)臨 (2)繰
6. (1)規 (2)視
7. (1)釈 (2)択
8. (1)拠 (2)処
9. (1)上 (2)土
10. (1)膨 (2)影
11. (1)頻 (2)順
12. (1)返 (2)反
13. (1)存 (2)序

理( )
零( )
( )板
( )旋
( )り返し
( )格
希( )
占( )
希( )
( )響
( )度
( )射
秩( )

( )送
( )拠
( )序
( )解
( )界
注( )
選( )
( )理
面( )
( )張
( )電圧
繰り( )し
依( )

Ex. 9.5   Sentence translations

1. 最近の分子線エピタキシー法による薄膜結晶技術の急速な発展に伴い、単原子層の厚さの程度の範囲で急激な組成変化を示し、電気的にも光学的にも極めて良質な半導体ヘテロ接合界面が作られるようになった。

2. その中には物質の互いに異なる単一層からなる超格子という極端な例もあり、また最近の超真空技術により、単一層からなる超格子の作成も可能となっている。

3. 単一ヘテロ構造においてももちろん近似的な波動関数が考えられる。

4. 一番簡単なものは三角ポテンシャル近似と呼ばれ、z＞0でのポテンシャルを一定の有効電場で置き換える。

薄膜	ハクマク	thin film	厚さ	あつさ	thickness
急速な	キュウソクな	rapid	急激な	キュウゲキな	sudden, rapid
発展	ハッテン	development, growth	良質	リョウシツ	good quality
			真空	シンクウ	vacuum
… に伴う	… にともなう	to accompany …	置き換える	おきかえる	to replace

Ex. 9.6   Paragraph translations

1. 酸化物超伝導体は、これまでに表に挙げてあるようなものが知られていたが、いずれも上の例のように鉛やチタンなど超伝導元素を含むものばかりである。これらの酸化物超伝導体は、電子密度が10^{19}–10^{21}電子/cm³で、金属間化合物超伝導体と比べて3桁近くも低く、しかもその臨界温度が格子欠陥濃度や組成に著しく敏感であるという特徴をもっている。一般に、縮退半導体での超伝導もそうであるが、低電子密度超伝導体の臨界温度は図のように電子密度とともに増加するので、酸素欠陥に起因する電子密度の微妙な変化により臨界温度が大きく変動するものと思われる。ところで、この表中のスピネル型酸化物$LiTi_2O_4$は、低温比熱などの測定からBCS理論で矛盾なく記述できる超伝導体であることがわかっているが、ペロブスカイト型酸化物である$SiTiO_{3-x}$や$Ba(Pb_{1-x}Bi_x)O_3$では、単一相の良質試料を作成することが困難なせいもあり、超伝導の起源などはまだ十分に理解されているとはいえない。

2. バンド理論では、一つの電子の運動に着目したとき他の電子の影響を平均的に考慮している。この近似では、一つの空間的状態には必ずスピン上向き・下向きの電子が同じようにはいることができる。しかし、電子間の相互作用、特にクーロン相互作用に従う斥力が強くなるとどうであろうか。このとき、電子は互いに反発して避け合う。この様子が、各格子点当たりの電子数が一個の場合について模試的に図に示してある。このようにクーロン斥力が強いと、各格子点当たりの電子の数が奇数個の場合、電子は自由に動くことができなくなり絶縁体となってしまう。こうして、バンド理論では金属的と予想される状況でもクーロン相互作用に起因する絶縁体状態が可能となる。これを、この機構の提案者の名前をとって、モット絶縁体と呼ぶ。酸化物の中にはモット絶縁体と考えられる例が多い。

3. 実例としては、GaAsとAlAs、あるいはGaAsと、AlAsとGaAsの合金AlGaAsからなる超格子の場合がこの図に相当する。この図のように、各々の半導体の伝導帯同士、価電子帯同士が重なり、エネルギーギャップの領域も部分的に重なって存在する超格子系をタイプIの超格子とよぶ。これに対して、一方の半導体の伝導帯と他方の半導体の価電子帯が重なるものをタイプIIの超格子とよぶ。InAsとGaSbからなる超格子がその例としてあげられる。

3桁	みけた	three orders of magnitude
組成	ソセイ	composition
敏感	ビンカン	sensitivity
縮退	シュクタイ	degenerate
微妙な	ビミョウな	subtle
矛盾	ムジュン	contradiction
困難	コンナン	difficulty, trouble
せい		result, outcome
着目する	チャクモクする	to direct attention toward

避ける	さける	to avoid
奇数	キスウ	odd number
予想する	ヨソウする	to predict
状況	ジョウキョウ	state of affairs
提案者	テイアンシャ	proponent
名前	なまえ	name
同士	ドウシ	fellow

(*Note*: When used as a suffix 同士 indicates a relationship between equals or counterparts.)

Translations for Ex. 9.5

1. Accompanying the rapid developments in recent molecular beam epitaxy thin film crystal technology, semiconductor heterojunction interfaces can be made that show sudden compositional variations in regions on the order of the thickness of a monoatomic layer and yet still have extremely high electrical and optical quality.
2. Among these are some that contain as their ultimate limit superlattices made from individual layers where each layer is a different substance, and the latest ultra-high vacuum technology is actually making possible the composition of superlattices from these single layers.
3. We are, of course, also able to think of an approximate wave function for a single heterostructure.
4. The simplest one is called the triangular potential approximation, and we replace the potential for $z > 0$ with a fixed effective electric field.

Translations for Ex. 9.6

1. Until now, as can be seen by what is given in the table, every one of the oxide superconductors has contained a superconducting element such as lead or titanium. These oxide superconductors have electron densities between 10^{19} and 10^{21} electrons/cm^3 which is nearly three orders of magnitude lower than for intermetallic superconductors. Furthermore, they are characterized by the remarkable sensitivity of their critical temperatures to lattice defect density and composition. Generally, it is thought that this is also true for superconductivity in degenerate semiconductors, and since, as shown in the figure, the critical temperature of superconductors with low electron densities increases with electron density, it is thought that subtle changes in the electron density caused by oxygen deficiencies could cause large variations in the critical temperature. $LiTi_2O_4$, a spinel type oxide that appears in the table, is known from its low-temperature specific heat and other properties to be a superconductor that is consistently described by the BCS theory. However, because perovskite oxides such as $SiTiO_{3-x}$ and $Ba(Pb_{1-x}Bi_x)O_3$ are difficult to fabricate in single-phase, high quality samples, we are unable to say that issues such as the origin of their superconductivity are adequately understood.

2. In band theory, when we direct our attention toward the motion of a single electron, we consider the averaged influence of the other electrons. In this approximation, it is always possible for spin-up and spin-down electrons to enter a single spatial state. However, what about when the electron-electron interactions, particularly the repulsive force from the Coulomb interaction, become strong? At that time, the electrons mutually repel and avoid each other. This aspect is schematically shown in the figure for the situation where the electron number is unity for each lattice point. When the Coulomb repulsion is so strong and the number of electrons per lattice point is an odd number, the electrons become unable to move freely and an insulator is formed. Thus, even under the conditions that could lead band theory to predict a metallic state, it turns out to be possible to have an insulating state brought about by the Coulomb interaction. Such a material is called a Mott insulator after the name of the person who proposed this mechanism. There are many examples among oxides that can be thought of as Mott insulators.

3. As a real example, the case of the superlattice formed from GaAs and AlAs or with GaAs and the alloy of AlAs and GaAs, AlGaAs, corresponds to this figure. As shown in the figure, there is overlap between the respective conduction bands and between the respective valence bands of the two semiconductors. A superlattice system where there also exists an energy gap region that is partially overlapped is called a type I superlattice. In contrast, one formed by overlapping a conduction band from one semiconductor and a valence band from another semiconductor is called a type II superlattice. An example of this is the superlattice formed by InAs and GaSb.

囲	イ かこ (む)	enclosing, surrounding to enclose, surround
円	エン まる (い)	circle round, circular
衝	ショウ	collision
総	ソウ	all; general
側	ソク −がわ	side side
退	タイ	receding, withdrawing
展	テン	expanding
薄	ハク うす (い)	thin, dilute thin
範	ハン	limit; model
備	ビ そな (える)	preparation to provide, equip

円　囲

総　衝

退　側

薄　展

備　範

囲

周囲	シュウイ	periphery, surroundings
範囲	ハンイ	extent, range, scope
雰囲気	フンイキ	atmosphere

円

円形	エンケイ	round shape, circle
円周	エンシュウ	circumference
円振動	エンシンドウ	circular vibration, circular oscillation

衝

衝突	ショウトツ	collision
電子・電子衝突	デンシ・デンシショウトツ	electron-electron collision
非弾性衝突	ヒダンセイショウトツ	inelastic collision

総

散逸総和則	サンイツソウワソク	dissipation sum rule
総計	ソウケイ	total amount, grand total
総合	ソウゴウ	general, comprehensive
総和公式	ソウワコウシキ	summation formula
電気伝導総和則	デンキデンドウソウワソク	electric conduction sum rule
電子技術総合研究所	デンシギジュツソウゴウケンキュウジョ	Electrotechnical Laboratory

側

内側	うちがわ	the interior, inside
外側	そとがわ	the exterior, outside
向こう側	むこうがわ	opposite side, opposing side

退

縮退度	シュクタイド	degeneracy
縮退半導体	シュクタイハンドウタイ	degenerate semiconductor

展

展開	テンカイ	expansion {math}
展示	テンジ	exhibition, display
展性	テンセイ	malleability
展望	テンボウ	view, outlook, prospects
発展	ハッテン	development, growth

薄

希薄な	キハクな	dilute, rarefied, thin, sparse
希薄溶液	キハクヨウエキ	dilute solution
超薄膜	チョウハクマク	super-thin film
薄膜	ハクマク	thin film, thin membrane
薄膜の超伝導	ハクマクのチョウデンドウ	superconductivity in thin films
薄膜の超伝導体	ハクマクのチョウデンドウタイ	thin film superconductor
薄膜の臨界磁場	ハクマクのリンカイジば	critical field in thin films

範

範囲	ハンイ	extent, range, scope

備

予備実験	ヨビジッケン	preliminary experiment
装備	ソウビ	equipment
設備	セツビ	facilities
準備	ジュンビ	preparation
整備する	セイビする	to equip, maintain, prepare

SUPPLEMENTARY VOCABULARY USING KANJI FROM CHAPTER 20

接触超微細構造	セッショクチョウビサイコウゾウ	contact hyperfine structure
相互作用	ソウゴサヨウ	interaction
偏差	ヘンサ	deviation, declination

EXERCISES

Ex. 10.1 Matching Japanese and English terms

( ) 範囲　　　　　( ) 整備する　　　　( ) 衝突の効果
( ) 内側　　　　　( ) 希薄溶液　　　　( ) 電子・電子衝突
( ) 外側　　　　　( ) 向こう側　　　　( ) フォノン衝突
( ) 準備　　　　　( ) 偏差　　　　　　( ) 非弾性衝突
( ) 展性　　　　　( ) 薄膜超伝導体　　( ) 電子技術総合研究所
( ) 円形　　　　　( ) 縮退半導体　　　( ) 電気伝導総和則
( ) 総合　　　　　( ) 総計　　　　　　( ) 散逸総和則
( ) 展示　　　　　( ) 円振動　　　　　( ) 縮退度
( ) 周囲　　　　　( ) 展望　　　　　　( ) 総和公式
( ) 円周　　　　　( ) 展開　　　　　　( ) 薄膜の臨界磁場
( ) 発展　　　　　( ) 超薄膜　　　　　( ) 薄膜の超伝導
( ) 薄膜　　　　　( ) 希薄な　　　　　( ) 予備実験
( ) 装備　　　　　( ) 設備

1. dilute solution
2. inelastic collision
3. round shape, circle
4. malleability
5. phonon collision
6. preparation
7. degeneracy
8. circumference
9. facilities
10. expansion {math}
11. summation formula
12. super-thin film
13. equipment
14. the interior, inside
15. general, comprehensive
16. dissipation sum rule
17. degenerate semiconductor
18. the exterior, outside
19. development, growth
20. extent, range, scope
21. effect of collisions
22. deviation, declination
23. exhibition, display
24. view, outlook, prospects
25. circular vibration
26. preliminary experiment
27. electric conduction sum rule
28. total amount, grand total
29. Electrotechnical Laboratory
30. electron-electron collision
31. opposite side, opposing side
32. thin film superconductor
33. to equip, maintain, prepare
34. thin film, thin membrane
35. superconductivity in thin films
36. periphery, surroundings
37. critical field in thin films
38. dilute, rarefied, thin, sparse

Ex. 10.2 Matching Japanese and English terms—names of Japanese organizations

The Japanese and English names of many organizations are not literal translations of each other.

( ) 計量研究所　　　　　　　　( ) 電子技術総合研究所
( ) 日本電信電話　　　　　　　( ) イオン工学センター
( ) 松下電器産業　　　　　　　( ) レーザー応用工学センター
( ) 科学技術庁　　　　　　　　( ) 日立中央研究所
( ) 環境庁　　　　　　　　　　( ) 地下無重力実験センター
( ) 工業技術院　　　　　　　　( ) 超高温材料研究センター
( ) 東芝　　　　　　　　　　　( ) 国際超電導産業技術研究センター
( ) 住友電気工業　　　　　　　( ) 生命工学工業技術研究所
( ) 日本物理学会　　　　　　　( ) 三菱電気
( ) 富士通　　　　　　　　　　( ) 理化学研究所
( ) 応用物理学会　　　　　　　( ) 新日本製鉄
( ) 日本電気　　　　　　　　　( ) 物質工学工業技術研究所
( ) 地質調査所　　　　　　　　( ) 無機材質研究所
( ) 気象庁　　　　　　　　　　( ) 機械技術研究所
( ) 特許庁　　　　　　　　　　( ) 金属材料研究所

1. Ion Engineering Center
2. Nippon Electric Co. (NEC)
3. Nippon Steel Corp.
4. Applied Laser Engineering Center
5. Matsushita Electric Industrial
6. Science and Technology Agency
7. Physical Society of Japan
8. Japan Microgravity Center
9. Toshiba
10. Patent Office
11. Meteorological Agency
12. Fujitsu, Ltd.
13. Environmental Agency
14. Geological Survey of Japan
15. Electrotechnical Laboratory (ETL)
16. National Research Institute for Metals
17. Institute for Chemical and Physical Research (RIKEN)
18. Agency for Industrial Science and Technology
19. National Institute of Materials and Chemical Research
20. National Institute of Bioscience and Human Technology
21. Hitachi Central Research Laboratory
22. The Japan Society of Applied Physics
23. National Research Laboratory for Metrology
24. National Research Institute for Inorganic Materials
25. International Superconductivity Technology Center
26. Sumitomo Electric Industries
27. Mitsubishi Electric Corp.
28. Japan Ultrahigh-Temperature Materials Research Center
29. Nippon Telegraph and Telephone (NTT)
30. Mechanical Engineering Laboratory

電話	デンワ	telephone	友	とも	friend
松	まつ	pine tree	富士	フジ	(Mt.) Fuji
-庁	-チョウ	agency	特許	トッキョ	patent
-院	-イン	agency, institution	中央-	チュウオウ-	central
東	トウ	east	国際	コクサイ	international
芝	しば	lawn, turf, sod	生命	セイメイ	life
住む	すむ	to dwell, live	菱	ひし	diamond shape, rhombus

Ex. 10.3 Choosing the correct KANJI

1.	(1)井	(2)囲	範( )		( )戸
2.	(1)円	(2)用	( )形		作( )
3.	(1)屈	(2)展	発( )		( )折
4.	(1)薄	(2)獲	捕( )		( )膜
5.	(1)衝	(2)衡	平( )		( )突
6.	(1)総	(2)統	( )計		( )合
7.	(1)範	(2)蔽	遮( )		( )囲
8.	(1)側	(2)則	規( )		外( )
9.	(1)透	(2)退	( )明		縮( )
10.	(1)備	(2)偏	装( )		( )光

Ex. 10.4 Sentence translations

1. 金属材料研究所では、20年以上超伝導材料、特に超伝導線材の研究開発に取り組み、表面拡散法によるV_3Gaテープ線材、青銅法による$(Nb \cdot Ti)_3Sn$極細多芯線材，イン・サイチュー法によるV_3Ga繊維分散線材などの高磁界用超伝導線材の実用化を図ることもに、レーザーや電子ビーム法を用いた新しい線材化技術を開発し、高磁界特性の優れた$Nb_3(Al \cdot Ge)$線材などの開発を行ってきた。

2. 新しいBi-Sr-Ca-Cu-O系高温超伝導体は、超伝導転移温度が初めて100Kの大台を越えたため、応用的観点から多くの注目を集めた。

3. Bi, Sr, Ca, Cu の成分比を変え、熱処理温度も変え、また溶融してみたり、雰囲気を真空、酸素、窒素中など、手を変え品を変えてもまだ曲線のテールにぶつかった。しかし、こちらの挑戦をあざ笑うかのように、たまには申しわけ程度に少し小さくなった。

取り組む	とりくむ	to struggle with, be engaged in		手を変え品を変えて	てをかえしなをかえて	using every possible means
青銅	セイドウ	bronze		ぶつかる		to bump up against
芯	シン	core		挑戦	チョウセン	challenge
多芯	タシン	multi-filamentary		あざ笑う	あざわらう	to mock, sneer
優れる	すぐれる	to excell, surpass		たまに		occasionally
大台	おおダイ	level, mark		申しわけ程度	もうしわけテイド	hardly worth mentioning
雰囲気	フンイキ	atmosphere				

Ex. 10.5   Paragraph translation

　　技術の選択に当っては技術分野を四つに大別した。それらは表に示すように、基本デバイス、回路およびシステム(A技術)、結晶(B技術)、プロセス(C技術)，デバイスの信頼性(D技術)である。まず、A技術であるが、バイポーラトランジスターは、このデバイスを使ったバイポーラ集積回路が歴史的に最初に世の中に登場したことと、現在でもこのデバイスがバイポーラ大規模集積回路のキーデバイスであることを考えると、まずこれを挙げるべきであろう。MOSダイオードは金属と酸化膜と半導体を使った電界効果デバイスであると同時に、現在の最先端のLSIであるDRAM(随時読み出し書き込み可能なメモリー)のメモリー機能がこのデバイスによっていることを考えると、これも落とすわけにはいかない。MOSトランジスターはバイポーラと並ぶ二大半導体デバイスであると共に、超大規模集積回路の最先端を走るMOSLSIのキーデバイスである。

大別する	タイベツする	to divide roughly	随時	ズイジ	at will, on demand
信頼性	シンライセイ	reliability	読み出し	よみだし	reading out
世	よ	world	書き込み	かきこみ	writing into
最先端	サイセンタン	most advanced	落す	おとす	to omit, drop

(*Note*: わけにはいかない is an emphatic expression used at the end of a sentence to indicate that the action mentioned immediately before is not acceptable or should not be done.)

Translations for Ex. 10.4

1. For more than 20 years at the National Research Institute for Metals, we have been engaged in the research and development of superconducting materials, particularly superconducting wire materials. In planning for the practical application of superconductor wire materials for use in high magnetic fields, we have developed V_3Ga tape made using a surface diffusion method, extremely fine multi-filamentary $(Nb \cdot Ti)_3Sn$ wires materials made using the bronze method, V_3Ga fiber dispersion wires made using the *in situ* method, and so forth. Besides that, we have developed new wire fabrication techniques using laser and electron beam methods, and are have been developing wire materials such as $Nb_3(Al \cdot Ge)$, which excel in their high-magnetic field characteristics.

2. The new high-temperature superconductor system Bi-Sr-Ca-Cu-O gathered a great deal of attention from the viewpoint of applications because its superconducting transition temperature was the first to cross over the 100 K level.

3. We changed the relative composition of Bi, Sr, Ca, and Cu, changed the processing temperature and tried fusing [the material]; we changed the atmosphere using vacuum, oxygen, and nitrogen; we used every possible means and still bumped up against the tail of the curve. Still, [the resistance] occasionally became slightly smaller by an amount hardly worth mentioning, as though [the material] sneered at our challenge.

Translation for Ex. 10.5

In the selection of technologies, we roughly divided the fields of technology into four groups. These are shown in the table as fundamental devices, circuits and systems (technology A), crystals (technology B), processes (technology C), and device reliability (technology D). First, with technology A we must mention the bipolar transistor, since bipolar integrated circuits that use this device were historically the first to appear on the world scene, and even now this device is the key device in bipolar large scale integrated circuits. The MOS diode is an electric field effect device that uses a metal, an oxide film, and a semiconductor. We cannot very well omit this device, since the memory function for the DRAM (memory that can be read out and written into at any time) of the most advanced current LSI technology depends upon it. The MOS transistor, which together with the bipolar transistor represent the two great semiconductor devices, is the key device in the MOS large scale integration that drives the most advanced very large scale integrated circuits.

APPENDIX A: SUPPLEMENTARY KANJI LIST

In Chapters 5-20 of BTJ you learned 365 KANJI, and in this volume you have learned an additional 100 KANJI. Still other KANJI were given in the vocabulary lists following many of the exercises. In this appendix, the more generally useful of these KANJI are listed in several categories. For the sake of brevity you will find here only the most important KUN and ON readings (marked with ▲) and JUKUGO. See also Appendix C for supplementary scientific and technical terms.

A.1: New KANJI that are used in several important words

演	▲演	エン	performance
	演算子	エンザンシ	operator {math}
	競演	キョウエン	competition
	講演	コウエン	lecture
簡	▲簡	カン	simple
	簡単な	カンタンな	simple
	簡約する	カンヤクする	to simplify
急	▲急	キュウ	sudden, steep
	▲急ぐ	いそ(ぐ)	to be in a hurry
	急激な	キュウゲキな	sudden, rapid
	急峻な	キュウシュンな	abrupt
	急速な	キュウソクな	rapid
広	▲広	コウ	broad, wide
	▲広い	ひろ(い)	wide
	▲広がる	ひろ(がる)	to spread out, widen
	広角度散乱	コウカクドサンラン	wide-angle scattering
剛	▲剛	ゴウ	hard, rigid
	剛性率	ゴウセイリツ	shear modulus
	剛体球	ゴウタイキュウ	rigid sphere, hard sphere
際	▲際	サイ	occasion
	実際に	ジッサイに	actually, in reality
始	▲始	シ	beginning
	▲始まる	はじ(まる)	to begin {v.i.}
	▲始める	はじ(める)	to begin {v.t.}
	開始	カイシ	beginning, start

斜	▲斜	シャ	slanting, diagonal, oblique
	▲斜め	なな(め)	oblique, slanting
	三斜	サンシャ	triclinic
	斜方	シャホウ	orthorhombic
	単斜	タンシャ	monoclinic
芯	▲芯	シン	core
	多芯	タシン	multi-filamentary, multi-core
底	▲底	テイ	bottom
	▲底	そこ	bottom
	基底状態	キテイジョウタイ	ground state
菱	▲菱	リョウ	diamond shape, rhombus
	▲菱	ひし	diamond shape, rhombus
	三菱	みつびし	Mitsubishi
	菱面形	リョウメンケイ	rhombohedral
	菱面体	リョウメンタイ	rhombohedral
並	▲並	ヘイ	being in a row, lined up
	▲並ぶ	なら(ぶ)	to be lined up
	並進	ヘイシン	translation {movement}
閉	▲閉	ヘイ	closed
	▲閉じる	と(じる)	to close
	閉じ込め	と(じ)こ(め)	confinement
	閉殻	ヘイカク	closed shell
	閉路磁区	ヘイロジク	closed-circuit domain
寄	▲寄せる	よ(せる)	to gather together, bring about
	▲寄る	よ(る)	to approach
	寄与	キヨ	contribution

A.2: KANJI pairs in which both KANJI are new

医療	イリョウ	medical treatment
改良	カイリョウ	improvement
概念	ガイネン	concept
括弧	カッコ	parentheses
興味	キョウミ	interest
国際	コクサイ	international
困難	コンナン	difficulty, trouble
手段	シュダン	means
住友	すみとも	Sumitomo
挑戦	チョウセン	challenge
提案	テイアン	proposal
凸凹	でこぼこ	unevenness
東芝	トウしば	Toshiba
任意の	ニンイの	arbitrary
背景	ハイケイ	background
博士	ハクシ or ハカセ	Ph.D.
富士	フジ	(Mt.) Fuji [in 富士通, Fujitsu]
矛盾	ムジュン	contradiction, inconsistency
予想	ヨソウ	prediction
歴史	レキシ	history

A.3: Vocabulary dealing with time

以来	イライ	(ever) since
今後	コンゴ	from now on
時刻	ジコク	time, occasion
従来の	ジュウライの	conventional
生命	セイメイ	life, lifetime
年	ネン	year
秒	ビョウ	second

A.4: Words and phrases in which one KANJI is new

挙げる	あげる	to mention, cite
著しい	いちじるしい	remarkable
意味	イミ	meaning
-院	-イン	agency, institution
印加する	インカする	to impress, apply
大台	おおダイ	level, mark
驚くべき	おどろくべき	astonishingly
書く	かく	to write

確認	カクニン	confirmation
片	かた	fragment
彼	かれ	he
奇数	キスウ	odd number
期待	キタイ	expectation
疑問	ギモン	doubt
鏡映	キョウエイ	reflection
近傍	キンボウ	neighborhood, vicinity
偶数	グウスウ	even number
桁	けた	digit, order of magnitude
厳密な	ゲンミツな	strict, close
拘束する	コウソクする	to restrain, constrain
考慮する	コウリョする	to think, consider
越える	こえる	to transcend, go beyond
幸いな	さいわいな	fortunate
避ける	さける	to avoid
撮影	サツエイ	photography
参照	サンショウ	reference
示唆する	シサする	to suggest
自身	ジシン	self
室温	シツオン	room temperature
凌ぐ	しのぐ	to withstand, surpass
純粋	ジュンスイ	purity
状況	ジョウキョウ	state of affairs
消滅	ショウメツ	annihilation
侵入	シンニュウ	penetration
垂直な	スイチョクな	perpendicular
姿	すがた	form
優れる	すぐれる	to excell, surpass
成功	セイコウ	success
青銅	セイドウ	bronze
世界的な	セカイテキな	global
節	セツ	paragraph
沿う	そう	to follow along
促進する	ソクシンする	to promote
素朴	ソボク	simple
探査	タンサ	investigation, probe
中央	チュウオウ	central
-庁	-チョウ	agency
電話	デンワ	telephone
同士	ドウシ	fellow
登場する	トウジョウする	to appear (on stage)
到達する	トウタツする	to attain, reach

特徴	トクチョウ	characteristic
特筆	トクヒツ	noteworthy
独立	ドクリツ	independent
特許	トッキョ	patent
名前	なまえ	name
に従って	にしたがって	according to
に伴う	にともなう	to accompany
残す	のこす	to leave behind
伸び	のび	extension
発揮する	ハッキする	to exhibit, demonstrate
浸す	ひたす	to immerse, soak
微妙な	ビミョウな	subtle
敏感	ビンカン	sensitivity
深さ	ふかさ	depth
付随する	フズイする	to accompany
普通	フツウ	usual, ordinary
振る舞う	ふるまう	to behave
分野	ブンヤ	field (of study)
隔てる	へだてる	to separate, interpose
便利	ベンリ	convenient
包含する	ホウガンする	to include, imply
母体	ボタイ	host body
満たす	みたす	to fill (up)
有名な	ユウメイな	famous
容易に	ヨウイに	often, well
呼ぶ	よぶ	to name, call
余分	ヨブン	extra, excess
略記する	リャッキする	to outline, sketch briefly
良質	リョウシツ	good quality
隣接	リンセツ	adjacent
論文	ロンブン	scientific paper
枠	わく	framework, frame

APPENDIX B: ON-KUN INDEX FOR THE KANJI EMPHASIZED IN THIS BOOK

The number after a KANJI indicates the lesson in which that KANJI is introduced. ON readings are given on this page in the GOJUU-ON order; KUN readings are given on the following page. The list of readings for dedicated KANJI pairs appears following the list of ON readings.

イ	依⁶維⁷囲¹⁰	ジク	軸⁶	ハイ	排³
イキ	域²	シツ	失⁵	ハク	薄¹⁰
イン	因¹引²	シャク	釈⁹	バク	縛⁷
エン	縁⁵円¹⁰	ジュウ	縦⁶	ハン	範¹⁰
オン	横⁶	ジュン	純¹順⁹	ヒ	砒¹
カ	荷³	ショウ	障⁴称⁷衝¹⁰	ビ	備¹⁰
カク	格¹拡⁷殻⁸	ジョウ	乗⁸	ヒン	頻³
カン	陥³感⁶緩⁶	シン	親⁶	フ	負¹
キ	規¹軌²希⁹	セイ	整⁸	フク	幅³
ギ	擬⁵	セキ	斥²	ヘキ	壁⁴
キャク	却⁴	ゼツ	絶⁵	ヘン	偏⁸
キョウ	鏡⁴	セン	選⁴繊⁷	ホ	保⁶
ギョウ	凝⁵	ソウ	走²双⁶操⁷総¹⁰	ボ	模⁷
キョク	局⁶	ソク	束⁷側¹⁰	ボウ	膨⁹
キン	均⁵	ソン	損⁵	メイ	鳴⁹
ク	区²	タイ	退¹⁰	モ	模⁷
グ	具³	タク	択⁴	モウ	網⁸
グン	群⁷	タン	短⁸	ユ	由³輪⁹
ケイ	軽²	ダン	弾³	ユウ	由³融⁹
ケツ	欠³	チョウ	張³	ヨウ	様⁵
ケン	顕⁴	テン	展¹⁰	ラク	絡⁸
ゲン	源⁸	ト	土⁹	リョウ	領²
コウ	格¹孔¹衡¹	ド	土⁹	リン	臨⁹
サ	査⁴	トウ	答⁵凍⁷	レイ	励²冷⁴零⁴
シ	思¹指¹止⁸紫⁸視⁹	ドウ	道²		

Dedicated KANJI pairs

いど	井戸¹	コテン	古典⁷	しきい	敷居⁸
エイキュウ	永久²	コウフク	降伏¹	ホカク	捕獲⁶
カンショウ	干渉⁷	シャヘイ	遮蔽⁸	マサツ	摩擦⁷
キカ	幾何³	センキョ	占拠⁹	ラセン	螺旋³
くりかえし	繰り返し⁹	チツジョウ	秩序⁹		

あな	孔[1]		たもつ	保つ[6]
あみ	網[8]		つち	土[9]
うしなう	失う[5]		ととのう	整う[8]
うすい	薄い[10]		ととのえる	整える[8]
えらぶ	選ぶ[4]		とまる	止まる[8]
おう	負う[1]		とめる	止める[8]
おちいる	陥る[3]		なく	鳴く[9]
おもう	思う[1]		なる	鳴る[9]
おや	親[6]		に	荷[3]
かがみ	鏡[4]		はしる	走る[2]
かく	欠く[3]		はば	幅[3]
かこむ	囲む[10]		はる	張る[3]
かべ	壁[4]		ひえる	冷える[4]
から	殻[8]		ひく	引く[2]
かるい	軽い[2]		ひずみ	歪み[5]
がわ	側[10]		ひやす	冷やす[4]
さす	指す[1]		まるい	円い[10]
さま	様[5]		みじかい	短い[8]
しばる	縛る[7]		みち	道[2]
そこなう	損なう[5]		むらさき	紫[8]
そなえる	備える[10]		ゆび	指[1]
たえず	絶えず[5]		よこ	横[6]
たて	縦[6]		よる	依る[6]

99

APPENDIX C: SUPPLEMENTARY TECHNICAL VOCABULARY IN SOLID-STATE PHYSICS

The following words were not formally presented in Lessons 1-10. They contain additional new KANJI, and may simply be learned as complete words.

閾	イキ or しきい	threshold
渦糸状態	うずいとジョウタイ	vortex state
音響的分枝	オンキョウテキブンシ	acoustic branch
加工硬化	カコウコウカ	work hardening
仮想結晶近似	カソウケッショウキンジ	virtual crystal approximation
貴金属	キキンゾク	noble metals
近藤効果	コンドウコウカ	Kondo effect
残留抵抗	ザンリュウテイコウ	residual resistance
刺激	シゲキ	stimulus
充填率	ジュウテンリツ	filling factor
消衰係数	ショウスイケイスウ	extinction coefficient
消滅演算子	ショウメツエンザンシ	annhilation operator
侵入距離	シンニュウキョリ	penetration depth (distance)
隙間	すきま	gap, interstice
正弦	セイゲン	sine (trigonometry)
生成演算子	セイセイエンザンシ	creation operator
成長核株	セイチョウカクかぶ	growth nucleus
摂動理論	セツドウリロン	perturbation theory
閃亜鉛鉱構造	センアエンコウコウゾウ	zincblende structure
塑性的	ソセイテキ	plastic
段丘状階段	ダンキュウジョウカイダン	terrace step
頂点	チョウテン	vertex
滴	テキ	droplet
出払い層	ではらいソウ	depletion layer
電池	デンチ	battery
伝播遅延時間	デンパチエンジカン	propagation delay time
伝搬遅延時間	デンパンチエンジカン	propagation delay time
刃状転位	はジョウテンイ	edge dislocation
バンド折畳み効果	バンドおりたたみコウカ	zone folding effect
表皮	ヒョウヒ	skin (effect)
不足型半導体	フソクがたハンドウタイ	deficit semiconductor
復素屈折率	フクソクッセツリツ	complex refractive index
崩壊	ホウカイ	decay, disintegration
補償	ホショウ	compensation
密度汎関数の方法	ミッドハンカンスウの方法	density functional method
量子補正	リョウシホセイ	quantum correction
ローレンツの空洞電場	ローレンツのクウドウデンば	Lorentz cavity field